"Speaking directly to C-level men and corporations, Teresa calls out systemic bias against women in the workplace, spelling out exactly what women think, while offering highly executable solutions for corporate and societal change. A must read!"

—Dianne Gubin, Co-CEO, C-Sweet

"Equal representation of women in c-suites and boardrooms is imperative for any organization, community, or culture to thrive. Suites and Skirts is a powerful reminder of the responsibility we all have, especially those currently in power, to be an ally, champion, and role model for challenging the status quo and driving change. Be bold, be loud, be inclusive."

—Brett Martinez, President/CEO, Redwood Credit Union

"A welcome fresh addition to any corporation's DEI initiatives. Challenging and what you would expect from a successful female CEO who has seen and lived it all. An opportunity to gain real perspective on what might not be working in your corporation, what the real barriers to women are and potential solutions...and not from another man but from a woman. And guess what...your shareholders might just thank you."

—Richard H. Cruickshank KC, Counsel, Dentons

"If this book doesn't motivate men to step up and relinquish power or women to push for faster change in the corporate arena, I don't know what will. This book eloquently yet boldly addresses the threads of the patriarchal fabric of Corporate America with clear reasons why their unraveling will result not in our demise but in our collective evolution. In this book, Teresa gives clear actions men should be taking today to play their part in moving humanity forward and it's high time they listen up."

—Cassandra Worthy - Speaker, Author and Corporate Consultant

SUITS AND SKIRTS

SUITS AND SKIRTS:

GAME ON!

The Battle for Corporate Power

TERESA FREEBORN

Redwood Publishing, LLC

Published by:
Redwood Publishing, LLC
www.redwooddigitalpublishing.com
Orange County, California

ISBN: 978-1-956470-68-0 (hardcover)
ISBN: 978-1-956470-69-7 (paperback)
ISBN: 978-1-956470-70-3 (e-book)

Library of Congress Cataloguing Number: 2022921656

Interior Design:
Jose Pepito

Cover Design:
Michelle Manley

Author Photo (on cover):
Ashley Barrett

For Frankie and Stella, who inspire me to do
my best to inspire them, every day.

CONTENTS

FOREWORD

Growing up, having a mom who was building a career wasn't always easy. At the time, my yearning for my mom to pick me up from school, to be waiting for me with fresh cookies when I arrived home, or to attend every single baseball game I played or performance I put on was very real. I was jealous of my friends with "stay-at-home moms." I didn't have a lot of friends whose moms worked as much as mine did, who went to the office early in the morning and did not come home until early evening, who had to travel across the country for business appointments, or who had dinner meetings and industry events that competed for her attention. So I felt I was missing something important a lot of the time. I wasn't able yet to understand that while I may have been missing something, I was gaining something as well. At that age, I never questioned where the abilities, curiosity, and courage that I demonstrated from an early age came from. I wasn't able yet to consider the source of my innate inclination to lead, my enthusiastically self-assured raised hand when my teacher asked, "Who wants to go first?"

Fast forward twenty-five years: two children, four degrees, and three careers later. I now run a successful business. I'm *Canada's Top 40 Under 40, Entrepreneur of the Year,* and CEO of a thirty-million-dollar company that my mom and I bootstrapped. I'm often asked on podcasts and panels how I had the courage to start a business. How did I have the confidence to make it all happen? I'm now able to articulate what I couldn't twenty-five years ago. Growing up, I was given the gift of a working mom. A mom who was a pioneer in a male-dominated finance industry in the eighties. A mom who sacrificed comfort and calm to accomplish big things. My mom didn't just tell me that I could be whoever I wanted to be and do whatever I longed to do; she showed me. She modeled confidence, she modeled tenacity, and, most importantly, she modeled passion. She showed me what it meant to get up every day and go after your dreams head-on. She wore shoulder pads, she left her children out of the office, and she had to be as masculine as she could be but just feminine enough so as to not rock the boat too much. She paved the way for women like me to invite our children into our work, to wear a sweatsuit on our Zoom call, to demand a seat at the leadership table. So I don't need to rock the boat. I set sail safely in the wake of working moms who have challenged the status quo before me. Moms like my mom.

It wasn't easy to get to this place. One of the biggest roadblocks for women to make it into the C-suites and boardrooms in business today is the underlying assumption that things are equal, a belief most commonly and strategically held by men. This is not a mindlessly held false assumption. There is more work to be done, a lot of work to be done. Men think because they have recently (and I mean recently) *let* women make decisions that our opportunities are now equal. This is a falsehood, perpetuated by white cis males everywhere. Let's be crystal clear so the men in the back can hear us: There is more work to be done. It will take decades to undo the centuries of structural oppression women have been made to endure. A conscientious effort to amplify women's voices is required and a steadfast commitment to undo the hyper-masculine corporate structures and cultures that celebrate male individualism and corporate advancement at almost any cost.

This book clearly states the daily soul-crushing issues facing women who are fighting for a seat at the leadership table and takes things one step further; it also outlines the solutions to these issues that will level the playing field quickly and fairly. It clearly illustrates how men, intentionally or not, hold women back in their career advancement and how they are the key to solving the inequity problem.

Some of you may view my mother's take on corporate inequality as being anti-men. That couldn't be further from the truth. Are men part of the problem? Yes. Are men a vital part of the solution? Absolutely. These two truths are not mutually exclusive. No one likes their flaws pointed out to them, but it is a necessary step on the path to change. You can't change and learn to do better if you don't know what behavior and thoughts need changing. I suggest that instead of getting defensive, you actually take a few moments and be self-reflective about the part you play in holding back women at work.

Letting us in to positions of power is a good thing. We bring different leadership skills to the table—not better or worse, just different. And these differences can be the difference between success and failure. I think the most important quality women bring to leadership is collaboration. Collaboration is Queen. Collaboration rules! Women work together, we ask for directions, and we have a propensity to uplift one another. We recognize that there is space for all of us. We recognize that we can cry and be vulnerable, and, at the same time, we can swiftly and efficiently make hard decisions. One does not exclude the other—this is a false dichotomy that only hurts one's ability to truly connect with our colleagues and teams in meaningful and altruistic ways. These connections are what help us gain broader perspectives and to get the most out of ourselves as leaders and our team members, effectively ensuring we come to the absolute best business decisions.

We can't make these business decisions if there is no equality and equity for women in leadership roles. We need someone who understands our challenges—and they *are* different than the challenges facing men. With women in leadership roles, other women know there is someone at the top who has their backs. I remember when I had my first baby. I was new to the US and didn't have any maternity leave. My boss was a woman. She held an executive title, and she had two kids. She lived my experience, so she worked with me to ensure I had a smooth transition back into the workplace and that I didn't feel like I was missing out on motherhood.

Young women professionals need women role models so they know that this is possible.

It goes without saying that women and men need to be equally represented in leadership roles. Women make up half of the population, yet we only hold 4 percent of leadership roles in Fortune 500 companies. This is gross underrepresentation of half of the population at the decision-making table, the table where they are making decisions that affect us, which, apart from being morally and ethically wrong, is just plain bad business. And bad business affects us all, exposing our economy and our very social fabric to unnecessary risk.

But all of that aside, women need to know that we can dream big and we can dream actively. Having women modeling what it means to be a woman and a leader makes it all more achievable. Equity in leadership means representation in leadership. Having more women at the table will ensure we will help close the gender pay gap, it will ensure policies favor both men and women, and it will encourage further diversity in the workplace. And finally, it will mean that young women will have women role models and mentors who understand their unique experiences and will help them more swiftly find a seat at the leadership table for themselves.

Listen to my mother. She has lived this. This is not theoretical for her or for other women. Men and women shouldn't be battling for corporate power; we should be sharing it.

Ashley Freeborn,
CEO, Smash+Tess

CHAPTER 1

Guys, You Have a
Woman Problem

G AME ON, GENTLEMEN. THERE IS A BATTLE FOR POWER AT ALL levels within corporations throughout the world. This battle is between you, "the suits," and women, "the skirts." Unlike the Sharks and Jets, who battled for neighborhood territory in *West Side Story*, the Suits and the Skirts are battling for power in the workplace. For a chance to move up the corporate ladder. For a chance at the boardroom table. For the same opportunities and positions of power that you already have—and are determined to keep for yourselves. Women make up nearly half of the workforce yet hold a small fraction of the positions of power and leadership. We've spent decades fighting for equality in the workplace, and the needle hasn't moved in any significant way. We tried playing nice and that didn't work; now, we're not going to be playing so nice anymore. We are demanding what we are due and parity is long overdue.

I'm about to establish unequivocally that there is a corporate problem of inequality, even if you don't think so. I'm going to show you how you consciously or unconsciously hold women back. And, more importantly, how to change this corporate culture. I will tell you many times throughout this book that having women in the C-suites and at boardroom tables increases profits. That is a fact.

Although company leaders, mostly suits, are generally reluctant to stick their necks out in support of or in opposition to anything controversial, the tide is turning. Research that I will discuss in greater detail later establishes that your customer base wants to see that you are keeping pace with the way they experience the world, not the way you might wish it were. They want to know that, on issues of gender, race, pay equity, and sustainability, you are on their side, that you can proactively co-exist in a changed world.

I think we can all agree that it's a confusing time for men and women in the workplace. For many decades, gender roles were clear and simple. Men were breadwinners and women were "homemakers," right? So how did we get thrown into the chaos we are experiencing now?

Until World War II, women were expected to be Domestic Goddesses, taking care of the home, having kids, making dinner, and doing the laundry. Then you needed us to help the war effort and fight the Nazis, so we became Rosie the Riveters. We were told to throw out our aprons and put on hard hats. Okay, put us in, Coach. We're team players.

Then, once the war was over, we were told to put down the hard hats and tie the aprons on again as if nothing had ever happened. That was a hard pill to swallow. It felt like we were taking a step back, but what could we do? For the next thirty years or so, women were relegated to clerk, stenographer, typist, or secretarial roles reporting to corporate men. Look pretty, be single, and type like a machine. Those were the requirements for success. No woman ever even conceived of becoming CEO of the company she worked at. That was just crazy talk.

Then, in the late sixties and into the seventies, all hell broke loose. Betty Friedan created NOW and the Supreme Court affirmed several laws protecting women in the workplace, from salaries to discrimination, to contraception, to Title IX. In 1963, Katharine Graham took the reins of *The Washington Post*. Mary Richards became a fictional TV producer at WJM-TV and turned the world on with her smile and her obvious ability. A host of trailblazing legislation and new laws were passed to help women get ahead in the workplace. Unfortunately, they didn't do much. All of those things were great, don't get me wrong, but we quickly discovered that legislation alone doesn't instantly end institutional prejudice and ingrained sexism, no matter what the law says. No matter how hard our Supreme Court and legislators worked to create equal opportunities for women in business, it just never caught on with those of you in positions of power. We were doing our part, pulling our weight, but that didn't seem to matter.

We filed, typed, organized, and took dictation *bigger, faster, and stronger* than anyone had ever done before. We were crazy good. We let our bosses know that we wanted more responsibility and proved we could excel at whatever was asked of us. We all thought we were on our way to becoming valued contributors at work. Then, our bosses decided that to progress, we needed more business education, setting up a new hurdle for us to get over. So, we got better educated—much better educated, it turns out—and began to move on. We started to make our way out of the clerk/secretary levels of business and into junior and middle management.

By the mid-eighties and nineties, we were making some serious inroads when it came to holding midlevel positions in most industries, but the Holy Grail—the senior executive table, the C-suites and boardrooms—remained elusive. And, unfortunately, those positions remain so today. We are constantly hitting a brick wall when it comes to getting that corner office on the top floor. Each time we chip out a brick in this wall, three more bricks are added. One step forward, three steps back.

When we talk amongst ourselves, some women question whether we are doing something wrong or are somehow inadequate, and that is what's keeping us in the metaphorical aprons and not the hard hats (i.e., C-suites and boardrooms). Although we have proven we can assume almost any job you need us to, many men now want to limit the jobs we are offered. No more hard hats, no more riveting. They want us to be satisfied with middle and upper-middle-management positions. That doesn't work for us anymore, yet we just can't shake the stigma(s) attached to being a woman in the business world. We have been busting our asses for decades earning our chance to lead, yet we are still forced to remain as followers. It's not from a lack of trying. It's not from a lack of ability. It's certainly not from a lack of drive and determination, and it is most assuredly not because we are not ready!

We are not the problem.

Guys, you are the problem.

The problem I am talking about, of course, is the lack of women in the boardrooms and C-suites of North American businesses. You men have been blocking our advancement in leadership roles for decades. You know as well as I do that involving women in decision-making is good for business. We've seen report after report in everything from the *Harvard Business Review* to *The Economist* to *Fast Company*, the *Wall Street Journal*, and countless academic papers—you name it—driving this point home. But, sadly this critical news falls on deaf ears.

When women are involved, businesses make more money.

So why are you so determined to lock us out? Maybe not you, personally, but many of your colleagues are. While they may not actively over-recruit men in order to maintain the status quo, you sure do not appear to be advocating for our advancement. The reality is that there are too few men willing to stick their necks out to help women get promoted. And without promotions, women can't move into corporate middle or executive management, C-suites, or boardrooms. In the last forty years, we women have received nothing but lip service when it comes to equal opportunities in your companies. There has been no substantive improvement. And we have had it. It is time you actually *did something* about this and not just *talked about* it. By "you," I mean men in general, as well as you personally.

If you have convinced yourself that *your* business does not have an equality problem, you are deluding yourself. You can tell yourself that all you want, but no one else believes you. Because the reality is that companies run by men rarely have an equal number of women in management. They are simply not there. Maybe excluding women wasn't a strategy or a plan, but it is the reality, nonetheless. And if you are not helping us move up in your organization, you *are* part of the problem.

Self-Made CEO

I am one of those women who successfully climbed the career ladder and landed one of those coveted CEO positions. I did very well in the corporate world, so I am not here to whine about being held back. However, I am virtually the exception. There are so many talented women who should already be in the C-suite.

I worked my way up from an entry-level role to a senior position in our local credit union. My parents gave me a strong financial footing from a young age, starting with extolling the benefits of joining the local credit union. They built solid relationships with virtually all of the staff at that credit union. I knew most of the people who worked there, too, because they regularly shopped at the Mini Mart next door, where I worked part-time during high school. I would greet and serve them as they came in to grab a coffee, a pack of cigarettes, or a gallon of milk.

Because I was friendly and helpful, could count money and make change, the folks at the credit union thought I would make a good trainee. I had proven to have basic commerce skills, which they appreciated. I was friendly and eager to develop relationships. So, when my mom inquired about a job for me after my graduation from high school, they were only too happy to extend an offer. Without even an interview, they agreed to hire me, starting the day after graduation.

My mom was much more excited about my new job than I was at that point, probably because I didn't know that I needed one immediately. I had kind of been looking forward to a few days of post-graduation relaxation and celebration before I had to start adulting. Guess not. I showed up ready to work that Monday morning.

I rose quickly in the ranks at the credit union thanks to my love of numbers, financial savvy, problem-solving ability, caring attitude, and work ethic. When I was second-in-command at the quickly growing branch office in my small hometown, I was offered and accepted a new job running a large branch of a credit union in downtown Vancouver, British

Columbia. The fellow I worked for was recruited to a CEO post at another financial institution and offered me the position of branch manager of their flagship branch, combined with the chief operations officer (COO) role overseeing another three branches. At this point, you might think I would have had my eyes on the CEO's job. But no. I did not, at all. I actually never imagined I could be CEO. With no female role models around me, my job, I quickly understood, was to make the CEO look good. And I was fine with that.

But I did recognize that I was good with numbers. So, when I was in my twenties and a high-school girlfriend suggested we pursue a college accounting degree, I thought it sounded like a good idea. I juggled night classes with work, a husband, and caring for two young children for two years before burning out. I was trying to do too much at once. I needed a break. I also wanted to spend time with my kids while they were young. School was interfering with that, so I put my education on pause.

Mothering my children was important to me, but I was also afraid that being a mom would overshadow being a COO, at least at work. I was very sensitive to that. To demonstrate to my employer how important my work role was to me, I took three months of maternity leave with my first but only three weeks of vacation with my second. Sure, maternity leave was available, but by my second child, I had realized that taking advantage of it would sideline me and put me on the mommy track.

By my mid-thirties, I had made it to the executive suite. I was a senior vice president at a much larger organization. It was there that I realized that to continue to progress beyond that role, I needed to go back to school. To be taken seriously, I needed the credentials and the credibility of a business degree.

By then, my two children were teenagers and still in need of oversight, so I applied to a two-year executive MBA program at one of the top business schools in Canada—Simon Fraser University. Through night and weekend classes, I could earn my MBA while holding onto my executive position and still have time for my kids.

Now, you may wonder how someone without an associate or bachelor's degree could be admitted to a master's program. I had an excellent GMAT score, a couple of years of accounting studies, impressive work experience, and executive responsibilities, so I pressed for admission without the requisite undergrad degree. They gave me the exception and admitted me to the master's program.

Most of my classmates were men. There were a few women, but not many. As with most MBA programs, we were divided into teams for regular group work. My team consisted of three male engineers and me. Although I was wary at first, this turned out to be a good mix of skills. Where they were strong in math and finance, I was strong in business planning, human resources, and sales, not to mention persuasion (given my success in talking the admissions office into letting me enroll despite my lack of an undergraduate degree). We did well.

Not that it was easy, because it wasn't. It was grueling. On top of being a corporate executive with a busy business travel schedule, I was also rearing two teens. To that, I added rigorous MBA coursework and my master's project. I felt I was enhancing my résumé through my growing work responsibilities and my educational credentials. Not many people could claim the same. I hoped it would position me for continued advancement.

Unfortunately, there were plenty of men who seemed to take pleasure in overlooking my qualifications and degree. As an executive, I frequently traveled to make presentations to various financial organizations (mostly CEOs and board members) to win support for new corporate initiatives. That meant I was almost always presenting to a room full of mostly older men.

After one presentation, I asked what questions they had for me, a senior executive. The first question was, "What is your phone number?" The next was, "Could you move farther away from the podium so I can get a better look at your legs?" And believe me, the behavior was not isolated to this one incident. It was a standard occurrence not just for me but as related to me by many other women in similar circumstances.

It boggled my mind—both that I would be treated so poorly as an executive and that other senior executives thought it was perfectly okay to sexualize a serious work engagement. No one in the room—my colleagues included—commented or told the guys off. It was amusing to them. It was ridiculous, yet all I could do in the moment was ignore them and laugh it off. Today, those types of Neanderthal comments made in public will get you fired, but it doesn't mean they don't happen behind closed doors. Women consistently do not receive the respect they deserve because apparently men do not yet feel we deserve it. They would rather comment on our physical features than the excellent strategic ideas we communicate and share. We are not taken seriously, no matter our performance or title. In your heart of hearts, you know I am not wrong, am I?!

At another meeting in one of our conference rooms, where my position and title (equal to theirs) were surely known to all in attendance, I entered and was asked by the senior-most man in the room if I wouldn't mind getting coffee for everyone. I turned right around and walked out. I sure as hell wasn't serving my colleagues—all of whom were men—coffee. I still wonder if they noticed that I didn't return. Something tells me they didn't.

Although there were many occasions where I was treated poorly because I was a woman, I didn't feel that I was ever actually held back. Because I didn't let others hold me back. I believed I could do anything I set my mind to and regularly attempted to advance my career in any way possible. Someone needed a volunteer for a high-profile assignment? I raised my hand. Job openings were announced that were above my current pay grade? I submitted my résumé. I knew I probably didn't have a chance, but I wanted the recruiters to become familiar with me so that I would be top-of-mind when something came along that was a possible fit. I took every opportunity to get face time with the people in charge. I was strategic as hell.

I was also gifted with executive sponsors. These were not formal mentors but men (no women) in positions of power who saw leadership potential in me and wanted to support my ambitions. Some were my bosses and others were leaders in other departments who noticed my drive and abilities. The only time I ever had a female boss was at my very first job. It was she who let me in under the tent and gave me a shot. From then on, I only had male bosses.

I thought all women were getting the chances I was earning. Turns out, not so much.

My friend Sandy is a case in point. She started out as a communications specialist straight out of a top-ranked MBA program and consistently outshone everyone on her team on projects. Clients loved her, her boss loved her, but her male peers were more jealous than appreciative of her good work. Although they all routinely received performance bonuses because of their exceptional teamwork, the men who worked alongside her didn't want her to leapfrog them career-wise. So, when group evaluations were conducted, they regularly rated her lowest. She wasn't, of course, but they wanted to push her to the bottom of the candidates for promotion. And they were successful, for a time. Until someone in HR revealed to Sandy what was going on. That would explain why her performance reviews weren't as dazzling as she expected or why her bonus wasn't as high.

Knowing that she couldn't expect to change the culture single-handedly, she took one of the many job offers she had received from one of her clients, where she then had the pleasure of being the client her former colleagues had to report to. The only way Sandy could move up was to move out first, leaving her former employer scrambling to replace her expertise. Expect that to happen more and more going forward. Women are fed up with their inferior treatment.

How Much Progress Have We *Really* Made?

Because I had men championing my career and encouraging me to aspire to ever-higher-level jobs, I thought my experience was universal—that women everywhere were being promoted and advanced by the men in their corner. I was sure that progress was being made. I made it to CEO, and

I have also worked directly for many CEOs in my career. I have recently spoken extensively with female colleagues who are at the executive table. Overwhelmingly, the consensus of these women who had years, sometimes decades, of executive experience were quick to say their experience and their skills are not as valued as their male counterparts. It was an eye-opener to see the world through their lens—the one that most women who aren't CEOs view it through. Was the lack of consideration for their ideas and perspectives because they were women?

I always counsel my female colleagues to pay very close attention and become more mindful of how things happen in an executive meeting or a board meeting. The nuanced difference between how a man's or a woman's perspective is received and by whom is surprising. The result is always the same. Their eyes are opened to the reality of how women were still regarded in these settings. Invisible and underappreciated, yet still doing much of the work for men who were taking the credit. I, and most women, believed that these kinds of situations were anomalies and that most women executives had the full support of their companies—that they were being promoted and were valued for their contributions to the C-suite.

Only they weren't. In fact, women clearly hadn't made much progress *at all*.

We've heard that younger generations view women differently today, which gives me hope that we might soon see some real progress. And then I hear recent stories like my niece Bailey's, and my cynicism returns.

Hired as an entry-level staffer at a local bar specifically because they had no women on the team and wanted a more diverse crew, twenty-something Bailey made an impression on management right away with her hard work and willingness to do whatever needed handling. Pick up used glasses left on tables? Check. Clean the women's bathroom? Check. Fill in to help wash glasses for the bartenders? Check. Her performance quickly had managers expressing appreciation and telling her they would soon promote her so she could start to learn how to bartend, she was such a good worker.

Sure, other men were hired after her, but she was at the top of the list for a promotion, they assured her.

And then Will, who was a later hire and generally a slacker, got scheduled for bartender training. Bailey was confused. So, she asked around about why she had been passed over. Her work was terrific, they confirmed, but the male managers just felt more comfortable around Will. Bailey began applying for jobs at other bars and immediately had multiple offers, including bartender training right off the bat. Turns out holding onto a top employee was less important to them than being able to hang out with the guys at work.

Not only is that bad news for women leaders, but it's bad news for men leaders who refuse to acknowledge the skills and expertise of the women in their employ. They're missing out in a pretty major way.

It's also bad news for companies that are treating women so poorly. Younger employees of all genders are noticing. They're seeing firsthand that companies don't value top employees, though it is evident that they value men more than women. This lack of employer loyalty may be among the several significant drivers behind declining employee tenure.

Workers don't stick around long anymore. Why should they? There's certainly no loyalty demonstrated toward them. So, when a better offer comes along, and believe me, they are watching for them, they're happy to jump ship and bring their years of experience with them somewhere else. They see how little women are valued, and they know the same may be thought of them, so they leave at the first opportunity.

Of course, women have been talking to other women about this for decades, commiserating amongst each other, trying to figure out what can be done. What they have—we have—discovered is that nothing has changed. There has certainly been a lot of talk, and a lot of talk makes one think that the progress is solid. But once you actually review the percentages of women in the C-suite and at board tables, you can quickly conclude otherwise. Brainstorming and networking with each other have gotten us nowhere (other than providing a forum of support) because we are not the ones in power. We are not the obstacle. We are not the problem.

It was through other women colleagues at an East Coast corporation that my friend Marie learned that she was being paid less than a male intern working in the mailroom. She was the secretary to the head of a major department at the corporation, bringing with her four years of an Ivy League education. The male intern was still in college.

When Marie asked her boss why she was being paid less than the intern, she was told, "That's just what your position pays." (You can almost picture him shrugging his shoulders as if to say, "Nothing I can do about it.") Yet there was and is something managers can do when they discover talented women are being underpaid with respect to men. They can adjust the salary range or give a one-time increase or promotion. It is not hard to even the scales, if you want to.

It has become starkly apparent to us that, as women, we need to be speaking to men and, specifically, men in positions of power. You men are the gatekeepers, the guardians, and the bottlenecks. That may not seem like a problem to you, but the truth is, leaving women out of senior positions puts your company at a significant disadvantage. When you only have men weighing in on decision-making, you're not getting the best ideas or the best results.

I guess if you do not believe that, then your reluctance to help women makes sense. After all, if you don't think women have a different perspective that may be useful to you, I get why you'd leave us out in the cold. It is not fair or right, but it certainly protects your position of power and provides a convenient, even if false, rationale for your behavior.

Or maybe you feel threatened. Maybe you recognize that the best ideas to come out of your organization were proposed by women, and you cannot have that. You might get passed over for promotion or, worse, replaced by a woman. So, you downplay the ideas, ignore them, or claim them as your own. Anything to cut women out of the picture and ensure you remain in it. You keep women out of the limelight, resigning them to their lower positions on the totem pole so they never have a chance to rock the boat.

The thing is that approach, simply stated, is stupid because it goes against your self-interest. The research is crystal clear: Elevating women into corporate leadership is good for business. Which means it is good for you, too. Companies with more women executives make more money. More money earned corporately rationalizes more compensation, more bonuses, and more career growth—for you.

Having women involved in making important decisions means the decisions made are better, smarter, and more profitable. And that's not just my opinion. In fact, I am going to overwhelm you with data to prove my point because many of you apparently do not seem to be listening to women at all. Perhaps you'll listen to male experts who echo what I'm telling you—to achieve higher corporate profits, higher ROI, higher ROA, better investor relations, more patents, and higher employee retention, you need women involved.

And the superior results are not limited to the corporate sector. Let's talk about government and educational leadership. Imagine what the world would look like if women held a proportionate share of leadership positions in other aspects of life. Would the conflicts we have today be raging? Probably not. Would fundamentals of life, like housing, childcare, and education, be higher priorities? Would communities and families be stronger units? My guess is they would be.

Which makes everything better for everyone.

And that confuses me and should interest you. If your life and those around you could be better and your family's life could be better, why the hell are you not with us? Now.

Women make a positive impact when they lead. Period. That does not mean men cannot lead, too, but we need to be working together, not as adversaries. And we can't do that until we get more women into those positions of power, influence, and decision-making. Only then can they make a positive difference. You need to help women do that.

Get Out of the Way

Now, maybe you aren't pushing for more female representation because you feel like we've made enough progress. You've convinced yourself women have already made good headway. Is that it?

Well, if you call an increase in the Fortune 500 of forty female CEOs over the course of fifty years headway, then I question your math skills. We've gone from one female CEO in 1972 to a grand total of forty-four female CEOs in 2022. Over fifty years! That is not improvement. That is ridiculous and pathetic and shameful.

And let us talk about women on boards. I do not care how you look at it or try to spin it, but when women make up only around 25 percent of all corporate board positions, we are never going to see major change. There are still too many boards of directors that have no women on them at all. And a whole lot more than that think having one or two is plenty, if not one or two too many.

The problem exists today because men are promoted into management positions far earlier in their careers; women are effectively left behind, according to McKinsey. When women are promoted into the ranks of management at far lower rates than men, that means there are far fewer women candidates available to be promoted into more senior positions on the career ladder. Just as there are few female senior managers to pull advancing corporate women up. It is a very real and negatively consequential kind of Catch-22. We need women in power to pull women up, but we cannot move any women up because there aren't enough in the executive pipeline.

The situation is even more dire for women of color. Their chances of moving into the C-suite have historically been virtually nonexistent. And I don't see that situation improving much going forward either unless something dramatically and structurally changes. For that to happen, we need your help.

Because what is blocking all women's advancement, regardless of race, creed, or color, is men, pure and simple. It certainly isn't women! We all know that women are just as ambitious, capable, charismatic, and statistically more educated than men in power. And yet, sometimes purposely and sometimes unwittingly, men are more supportive of men's promotion and career advancement than they are of women's. Men are more comfortable advocating for people like them, meaning other men. It almost seems like there is a corporate bro code in place.

Granted, women do the same, trying to pull their female subordinates up when they can, but with fewer women in the senior ranks (the pipeline), it is an uphill battle. Until men are willing to jump in and provide some assistance, it will continue to be challenging to push or pull women into more senior corporate roles and close the executive gender gap.

Ironically, men are both the problem and the solution. Where male Baby Boomers were only accustomed to interacting with women in the workplace as secretaries and underlings, more recent generations, starting with Gen X up through Millennials and Gen Z, are starting to recognize the value that women in positions of power offer employees and employers. A research study I commissioned, and which you will hear more about in the coming chapters, confirmed this.

Maybe because they were raised by strong women, younger men recognize and understand that women in top positions do add value to businesses. We bring a special set of skills to leadership positions that men will never have unless, of course, they actually work with and interact with women on a daily basis. Men also need to be prepared to accept the way we manage and get things done and learn from us. Yes, our leadership style may be different, but that does not make it inferior. You are not the only experts on leadership, believe it or not. Yes, we know that women lead differently. In fact, in study after study, those differences show we lead better and more effectively than you. Give the women in your company a chance to prove that to you and you will be impressed with the positive changes you see.

But without the support of men in executive and feeder positions, we can talk about it until we are blue in the face and nothing will ever change. This lack of support underscores why women are starting their own businesses in droves. We are getting tired of being overlooked and underappreciated. And if you will not help us get a seat at the C-suite table, not only will you miss out on our superior leadership skills, but you may encounter some new competitors who are itching to take you on.

Those competitors are capable women who are giving up on climbing the corporate ladder and are striking out on their own in record numbers. More than 5.4 million new businesses were established in 2021, with nearly 50 percent belonging to women, cloud software company Gusto reports. That's a record number of women-owned start-ups, up from 28 percent in 2019.

However, self-starting female entrepreneurs are a relatively new species. After all, it wasn't until 1988 that the Women's Business Ownership Act was signed into law in the US, making it possible for women business owners to apply for business loans without a male relative as a co-signer. We're still ramping our businesses up, but you can see that we are already making solid headway. Since you men won't let us in, many women are deciding to go it alone.

My good friend Ellen is one. After beginning her career in a high-powered law firm and quickly realizing she would not be given the same opportunities as her male colleagues, she quit and started her own firm. She gave up a hefty paycheck to call her own shots and is so thankful she did. Her business is now a multimillion-dollar coaching business with dozens of employees.

Look, guys, we women have been doing our part to gain the education, experience, and knowledge we need to move up the ladder into leadership positions for decades. So now it is time for you to go back to school, so to speak, and unlearn some very bad habits and prejudices. You need to tank a lot of erroneous assumptions you've been lugging around for years. You need to re-learn how to treat us women equally and fairly—to treat us like you treat the guys. It is time for *you* to do the hard work to reverse some really outmoded ways you think about and treat women in your workplace. Remember Helen Reddy and "I am woman, hear me roar, in numbers too big to ignore..." We are watching you like hungry hawks. Ignore us at your peril.

That is what this book is about. It is about recognizing the situation we are in and strategizing how to effect meaningful, quantifiable change. As a man, we need you to play a much bigger role in making this happen.

JUST THE FACTS, SIR.

- McKinsey research found specifically that "company profits and share performance can be nearly 50 percent higher at companies with women well represented at the top."

- McKinsey data from 2019 found that companies that are more gender diverse are 25 percent more likely to achieve above-average profitability versus companies with less gender diversity.

- That the first-ever female CEO of any business occurred back in 1889 when Anna Bissell assumed the CEO role following the death of her husband and propelled the company to international fame.

CHAPTER 2

Dude, You Are Stepping on My Skirt

T HERE ARE VERY FEW WOMEN IN THE C-SUITE AND EQUALLY AS FEW women around corporate board tables. This embarrassing state of affairs underscores the disproportionate distribution of power in corporate leadership. This situation is a fundamental and irrefutable corporate issue. Men in particular seem to be oblivious, indifferent or, worse, overtly obstructive in matters relating to the advancement of women.

Even well-intentioned men attempting to address the obvious disparity in opportunities for women are not able to grasp the true nature and extent of what is required to make meaningful changes in corporate organization and the male-centric mindset. These changes would create an environment where women would have unfettered access to compete for senior positions in business organizations, utilizing the same metrics by which men are assessed and allowed to advance.

By way of a recent example, while attending a global women's leadership network at a major conference, I was asked to meet with two senior leaders, both of whom were men. My immediate impression was that they were well-intentioned and enthusiastic about taking progressive steps that would advance women executives to the highest corporate offices in their industry.

They wanted my thoughts regarding a possible regional conference for women in their industry. They were also interested in my possible involvement in some capacity, perhaps as a presenter or as a facilitator of a panel of women speakers.

They felt that a women's conference might assist in elevating local women executives out of their current roles as glorified tea servers, figuratively speaking. They were open to and eager to see women take on decision-making responsibilities in top positions alongside their male counterparts. However, they were not convinced that the women they wanted to elevate had the self-confidence or self-assurance to assume that extra responsibility. They thought such a conference could be helpful: by giving them assurances that the women participants would, as a result, be ready and able to take on these new roles. They also wanted to outline strategies to prepare these women for fast-track advancement to higher-value work in the top executive ranks of their organizations.

I told them candidly, "It won't work." I explained that the issue was much more complicated than simply addressing a room full of women eager to hear how they might move up in the corporate ranks. The issue is complex, as is the solution, primarily because men created the male-centric corporate structure. Any attempt to alter that male-centric structure continues to be perceived as being undertaken at the "expense of men."

They simply needed to understand that the shift that needed to occur was not with women, but with the men and their erroneous perceptions of women's capabilities and capacity to do the work. Men need to be told to relinquish their outdated, culturally biased, and sexist views of women and take active measures to move women into senior-level jobs. Women's performance in those roles will be the litmus test.

The actual problem was that men could not see how they could help women advance into senior leadership roles because they were immobilized by long held but erroneous assumptions about women in the workplace. So, in this instance, words, although well intended, without action would do nothing to advance the process of bringing women into meaningful roles in senior management. The solution is found in deliberate action.

I didn't want to dampen their enthusiasm for tackling the problem, but what was clear to me was that they needed a women's perspective to understand that women didn't need their female peers counseling them. They needed to hear from men about what they could do to position themselves for advancement. They needed men's sponsorship and support, but mostly, they needed action. So, women are not the problem, just as the men in power are at the center of the solution.

In my mind, these men were metaphorically stepping on the skirts of the women they claimed to want to help. Instead of holding women back, if they would only lift their foot and assist women in being all they could be, they would start to see many more women move into leadership roles.

These seasoned senior leaders are stepping on women's skirts. It's a global phenomenon that needs to stop.

How Men Block Women's Advancement

To put it bluntly, the major roadblock to women's success at work is men's lack of advocacy for them. When you speak up on behalf of a woman at work, you are helping her advance. But lack of advocacy is just one example of a roadblock. Here are several more you should be aware of and that you can help remove. Included is a lot of discussion surrounding the different aspects of family and childcare. There's a lot to discuss because it is a common and heavy burden for many women. There are other roadblocks that are not family related that I will discuss, as well.

Clinging to the old work/family narrative. Guess what? We women can have children and still be great at our jobs. I know. Shocker.

Between women and men, women are by far the better multitaskers—a much researched notion and generally well-demonstrated fact. We can be great employers and employees and great parents simultaneously. However, the myriad additional roles and responsibilities women are typically expected to carry are burdensome, simply because most men do not want to do the unpaid, but nonetheless essential, work involved in running a household. Add to that being a parent with all that requires, and you can readily understand why women are highly motivated to be capable organizers of time and effort. Expecting women to be simultaneously employees, mothers, wives, caregivers, students, volunteers, etc., creates an enormous challenge for women and is the root barrier keeping women from successfully advancing through a corporate hierarchy. Expecting women to do everything related to home and childcare is very 1950s. It is outdated and obsolete and has no place in this new century.

On the flip side, if men are not going to step up (and by and large, they have not), women should not be penalized for doing what needs to be done in support of our families. Again, we are fully capable of walking and chewing gum at the same time. It is because men frequently opt not to be responsible for a full 50 percent of home and childcare that we step up to do what is needed. It is out of necessity. It is not because we said we *only* wanted to be wives, partners, and mothers. If we so choose, we want to and can be spouses, partners, moms, *and* leaders at work.

Because many male employers believe we must make a choice between family and career, we end up taking lateral promotions, getting off the fast track, going part-time, or shifting to roles that require less travel for a short time while we settle into new parenthood. But any suggestion that we may need a little grace while we adjust to our new circumstances has somehow been perverted to the notion that we don't want to work, or that our careers are less important, or, even worse, that the now-debunked maternal instinct is the driver in our lives.

Nonsense. That's just wrong! Too often, the end result is that our careers get derailed. We are made to suffer in terms of power, status, and income with those sacrifices we are compelled to make because most men won't share the burden.

This expectation that women should be the ones to compromise their careers in the name of family emerged decades ago when men were the de facto breadwinners and women the stay-at-home spouse or, if at work, the underling assistants. That was decades ago, pre-dating the Second World

War. Today, the reality is most families need two income-earning parents simply to meet the cost of living, yet it is the woman who is *still* expected to take on more than her fair share of the so-called "domestic" responsibilities. Women spend, on average, between three to six hours per day caring for others in unpaid care activities, while men spend an average of thirty minutes to two hours per day. Even the most-involved dads do less than the least-involved moms.

Men who run corporations apparently see no problem with this. And why would they?! Women shouldering the primary burden of childcare does not negatively impact anyone but themselves. It does not slow the progress of men on the payroll. In fact, it enables it. Less competition. How handy.

Valuing overwork. Another challenge for women is being expected to work long hours and weekends alongside their male colleagues who don't have the same caregiving responsibilities. Overwork is harder for us. Even if we wanted to work more, we typically can't because there is no one to handle our responsibilities at home. We are left holding the bag. It sucks, and it damn well is not fair.

Not that long hours are good for anyone, honestly. The belief that working long hours is good for productivity has been ingrained in many corporate cultures, despite the fact that overwork has been proven to decrease productivity and performance and increase sick time across the board. Many studies have confirmed that employee productivity is much higher when working forty hours or less a week versus working more than fifty. More hours at work actually diminishes productivity!

I had a great boss who used to say, "If we cannot get it done in the forty hours a week we should be working, we either planned poorly or it can wait until Monday." Great boss of an extremely successful company and a great way of thinking about work. Managing properly means that, with very few exceptions (and there *are* exceptions), no one should have to be up all night at work or be putting in a sixty-hour workweek to get the job done. Period. Instead of working employees to death, how about asking the people doing the work how long a project will take and plan accordingly. Or, as a suggestion, hire more people!

The major reason that overwork puts women at a disadvantage to their male colleagues is that men can often shift their non-work responsibilities to the women in their lives. We, on the other hand, often have no one willing to take on our family responsibilities. So, we take a step back in our careers when we can't keep working every weekend. Perhaps if there were more women in decision-making roles, this notion that overworking is a hallmark of best corporate practice, and the resulting so-called "performance" imbalance favoring men, would have been a thing of the past a long time ago.

Refusing equal childcare responsibility. As I touched on above, being saddled with the majority of childcare responsibilities is another cultural problem for women that critically impedes our career progress. Think about it. When a couple has a baby, how often does the father ever take paternity leave? Taking advantage of that benefit, if available, would allow his wife to go back to work immediately and reduce any career backlash she might face. But men who take paternity leave are as rare as you getting a hole-in-one. It happens, but not very often.

The only time in a woman's career when long hours are possible is before children arrive or after they're grown and flown. But when kids are in the picture, it is Mom who is expected to be the primary caregiver. That fact is almost always invariably career-restricting.

How did *I* do it? I call it my Mary Poppins story. When I was pregnant with my first child, I wondered if it might be possible to hire a nanny. Someone who could be me when I was busy with work. The only nannies I was aware of (aside from Mary Poppins) were for the very affluent. Daycares were prevalent, but I knew that shuttling my babies to and from the daycare and having to worry about pick-up, with the possibility of late afternoon/early evening work commitments and traffic delays, would make that type of arrangement less than ideal. Really, I had to figure out how to have a nanny. When I ran the numbers, I saw that 70 percent of my net take-home pay would go to pay for the nanny. It made no sense financially unless you factored in visions of a big career. And I did. I convinced my husband. I hired a nanny.

Do the kids themselves hold women back? Not really. I would say it is fathers who hold women back because of their unwillingness to share childcare responsibilities equally. A recent study concluded that in excess of two-thirds of men do not expect to equally share child-rearing and home-making responsibilities. What kind of nonsense is that? I mean, it took two to tango to make the child, it should take two to raise the child—equally. Science reminder: Women do not fertilize their own eggs.

My first marriage ended because of my career intentions. We found ourselves in irreconcilable positions. Although I respected his life plan, I was intent on attempting to achieve mine. Once my children were teenagers and more independent, I saw the opportunity to earn my MBA. My husband was planning for early retirement at fifty-five, and here I was, wanting to go to graduate school. Yet it wasn't until I turned forty that I finally had the opportunity to kick-start my career by first obtaining my MBA and then deliberately pursuing the CEO track.

You will often hear women say, "In my next life, I want to come back as a man." And, why not? Men reportedly are more satisfied with their careers: Their work is meaningful, they feel professionally accomplished, have plenty of growth opportunities ahead of them, and feel their work and personal lives are compatible. Yeah, being a man sounds like a great life. Definitely a different kind of gig than the one women are expected to show up for.

I think it is important that men understand that our career and success expectations were no different when we were starting our careers than yours were. Because of our extra responsibilities, we get penalized when it comes to career advancement. We still have the same career goals that we had and you have. What we don't have is the same opportunity.

And men, now that you have been given all the reasons why women need to and should accomplish their career aspirations (just like you), take my advice. While we are climbing those corporate ladders, support us in every way possible. If we have to travel more than you would like, accept it—it's part of the job description, not a vacation. If we have to attend a mostly male conference, trust us. If we have to have a drink with the guys after work, big deal. If we have to go golfing with the guys on a Saturday morning, so be it. Or if you are forced to grudgingly attend a dinner or event as our significant other, get over it. Remember, we've attended dozens of yours. It is hard enough for us to break into these male-dominated networks without having to be overly concerned about your feelings on these issues. We do not need an unnecessary layer of guilt. The job is hard enough.

Women who take maternity leave are penalized. Men often use maternity leave as an excuse to keep their foot on our skirts. The corporate world has much to improve upon with regards to providing generous maternity (and paternity) leave. Sadly, even with the current limited benefit, there is a significant penalty for actually taking advantage of that offered leave.

The longer women are away from work, the harder it is to get a promotion or a raise. The *Harvard Business Review* confirms this, reporting, "Evidence from a variety of countries reveals that the longer new mothers are away from paid work, the less likely they are to be promoted, move into management, or receive a pay raise once their leave is over. They are also at greater risk of being fired or demoted."

Part of the problem is that we are not visible while we are away from work. But the bigger issue is that employers interpret women taking maternity leave as signaling that our work is not important to us as it is to our male counterparts or that we are not committed to our careers. Are you kidding me? Do you think that when one of your buddies has a child, he no longer wants to be CEO? Why do we need to choose? Why can we not have both?

Then, of course, there is a different kind of penalty for *not* taking a maternity leave, which is that we are then perceived by friends and co-workers, men and, sadly, women alike, as being insufficiently maternal or not really committed to our families.

We are damned if we do and damned if we don't.

Having the capability to give birth does not mean that all women want to, and those who do are aware that they may be damaging their careers by having children. But they do anyway because having a family is important to them personally, essential for any economy to sustain itself and grow, and is central to the cultural imperative in most societies. It does not mean that a woman suddenly becomes any less talented, experienced, or committed to her work. The two can actually co-exist. You need to reframe how you think about women and motherhood as it relates to business, the economy, and our social fabric.

Men are uncomfortable socializing with women they work with. We have all heard that to succeed in business, "It is not *what* you know, but *who* you know," or at least that's how the old saying goes. That fact puts women at a distinct disadvantage when you men are unwilling to invite female counterparts and colleagues to join your social networks. I don't know why, exactly, but you guys frequently feel uncomfortable spending time one-on-one with women you work with. As a result, you exclude us from corporate dinners, golf outings, and other outside-of-work activities or events, which then effectively blocks us from developing vital relationships with potential mentors, senior management, or others higher up in the corporate hierarchy of the organization, thereby undermining our chances for advancement. You freeze us out, and even though sometimes it may be unintentional, the impact remains the same.

Informal networking events that men participate in strengthen personal and professional bonds, giving men a leg up in their careers. It's unfair because, generally speaking, women aren't welcome. The solution is to prioritize inclusivity. Include women in client meetings, encourage us to volunteer with organizations you are involved in, invite us to join local boards you are on, and take us to coffee or lunch to talk about our ambitions and career plans just as you do with your male subordinates.

If you think back on recent meetings, after-work activities, or other events and you cannot think of one woman who was in attendance, do you wonder why that is? Are you at all curious? And are you prepared to think about what you can do to fix that?

When I have asked men this question over the years, the usual response has been, "Well, I asked them and they turned me down." In other words, the men did their part—they asked. But we both know why she didn't accept the invitation: family commitments, daycare, medical appointments, soccer practice, music lessons, dance lessons, and the list goes on and on. They probably wanted to say "yes" but couldn't. So, what to do? Please keep on asking, and if you can give more advance notice with the invite, the women in your organization will be grateful, and they will find a way to say "yes."

If you can try to put yourself in the place of the women on your team, with all that they have to manage before and after work, it may sink in why they don't jump at the chance to grab drinks after work or stay late for a professional development session. The truth is, they would love to take you up on your offer. And if reading any of this has helped you see things from their perspective, how about pitching in a little more on their behalf and finding ways to make things work?

How to Become an Advocate for Women

Despite all the challenges that women face as a result of men's attitudes, there is a rising percentage of men who want to be progressive and supportive. They want to be part of the solution. These are the men who have come to recognize the value they and their companies get from hiring women in meaningful and impactful decision-making positions.

The problem is that there are also legions of men who are nervous about working alongside women. Not to get political, but the former US vice president Mike Pence refused to dine alone with women or to attend events where alcohol was being served and women were in attendance without his wife. This was apparently to avoid even the appearance of impropriety, as if women were going to purposely put him in compromising positions. Yes, the vice president. We assume this behavior is intended to demonstrate what a stand-up, principled fellow Mr. Pence is, but the subtext reads simply that men like him (and so, of course, all right-thinking men) need to be very mindful of scheming women intent on creating a situation of advantage by compromising them. Again, perhaps not an intended consequence but one that plays out at the expense of women, nonetheless. Oh, and it's just plain creepy.

If you think like this, you have no business even coming out of your mom's basement, much less being in a senior leadership role. You have a great deal more to learn about being a leader in today's world. We women want to work. We want to move up the corporate ladder. We do not want to date or marry you. Get it?! If you are capable of remaining completely professional in your dealings with other men, I have confidence that you can remain completely professional in your dealings with women, as women will remain professional in their dealings with you. If you cannot, you need to look for a job at a men's prison.

I am making such a fuss about this issue here because corporate networking is a critical element of the process of corporate advancement. Women need to be let into the conventional men-only social circles in order to get a foothold. That includes social club memberships, casual meals, drinks after work, industry conferences, continuing senior management development, and, dare I say it, sporting events and golf outings. And women are regularly excluded. Although I golf better than a lot of men I play with, I rarely get invited to golf with the boys. So, apparently, it isn't because I don't know how to play the game. And I certainly don't slow the men down, if you can appreciate the irony of the metaphor.

Sometimes the obvious exclusion borders on ridiculous. A company I worked for sponsored a charity golf tournament years ago. I had a conflict, so I declined the invitation and asked other senior managers (women and men) to indicate their interest in being part of a foursome at the tournament so we could be represented there. After the event was held, I found out that the team we sent consisted of four men who all regularly golfed together. Not only did they exclude women in the company from participating, but they did not even take advantage of the chance to mix and mingle with executives from other companies who were there. Not very strategic. And a wasted opportunity, but boys will be boys.

Unfortunately, this was not surprising, but it was disappointing since we had a number of competent women golfers on our corporate team. I reached out to ask the women if they were invited and, if so, why they did not choose to play. Their responses were simple and predictable. Some were simply not asked, and others who were asked could not imagine being away from their job for six hours on a workday; they were genuinely worried about shirking their responsibilities and deadlines. They were also not keen on the fact that the event continued on through the evening with a banquet and even more networking when they had families to get home to, especially when they hadn't been given sufficient notice to make arrangements on the home front.

What I do when I'm in such male-oriented golf situations is always ask to be placed in a foursome with people I do not know yet rather than people I see every day. (I am not sure why men decide to hang with their buddies versus seeking new business relationships during these events. Isn't that kind of the point?) Then, I simply beg off early to get home (which I always do). Since I have spent the day getting to know three strangers, it is never a bust in terms of networking, and I feel I have done what my company would want me to do at that point.

However, when it comes to women's networks, they are not working in terms of career progression.

This should not be a surprise to anyone since women's networks are predominantly made up of women and men's networks are predominantly made up of men. Well, guess whose network has the more powerful and influential members? Correct! Men. Because of this, women have a smaller pool of high-status women contacts on which to draw, not to mention that women have fewer ties to powerful, high-status men. In short, we do not have access—on a one-on-one level—to the people who can most readily make something happen for us.

Listen, men, you *must* include women in your corporate networks if you want to help achieve gender parity. You should be including women in your exclusive fraternity simply because it is in your own best interest. For decades it has been known, based on countless unimpeachable studies, that with women involved at a senior level in a company, it is significantly more likely to grow, prosper, realize, and retain its full economic potential. To get better business results, you need women at the table and in your networks.

Women's networks have been great for creating lasting relationships with other women. But the truth is, as stated earlier, women's networks tend to yield fewer leadership opportunities, provide less visibility for their leadership claims, and generate less recognition and endorsement. And what is the point if that visibility is only apparent to other women who are equally low on the corporate organization chart? The answer is: There is no point. And men already know this.

Certain executive positions in some industries are just plain harder for women to break into. In the financial services sector, for example, if you are in a sales position, such as mortgage production, you'll find far more men than women. It is all about the "booze schmooze." It is understood that dinners and drinks, sporting events, and male bonding are generally required to get the sale. And if women want to get their fair share of the business, they are going to have to find ways to participate in these kinds of activities. That said, it is of interest to note if women were on both sides of the mortgage production equation (the purchase and the sale), the end result would be the same but there would be far fewer hangovers.

Moreover, if women were in charge of setting up those schmooze sessions, they would be over in less than an hour, having served food along with the drinks while at the same time providing childcare for parents who are responsible for picking up their kids right at 5:00. They would also likely be much more productive and useful than the experience of simply getting drunk together!

Of course, the flip side is that men speak openly about the hunt and the conquest. Women have accepted that is how business is done in this sector, but they do not feel very good about it and do not agree that approach is necessarily the most productive. They also frequently feel guilty about how they have chosen to spend the night out versus spending time with their families. As we have already seen, there are too few husbands and partners willing to stay home to make dinner, clean the kitchen, handle bath and bedtime, and homework with the kids in support of their wives.

Women Leaving Corporate Jobs, and Why

An emerging but simple truth: If you do not learn how to integrate us into the corporate culture, we will go from team player to competitor. We will take our Chanel purses and walk out in our Louboutin stilettos and start our own companies. It is already happening all around you, so watch your back. You still have time; instead of creating a competitor, you should create an ally. But to create an environment of productive co-existence, here's what you need to know first.

The inherent lack of flexibility in the corporate workplace for women is a significant and ongoing problem. We all want challenging work, access to skill development, and a work environment in step with our multifaceted lives. Since women continue to do most of the emotional labor (nurturing of children and holding families and community together) and unpaid work at home, it is essential that challenging work also comes with an element of flexibility that recognizes that reality. That is why more and more women are taking their careers into their own hands with the startup of women-owned small businesses. The number of women-owned startups skyrocketed during the pandemic, as becoming entrepreneurs seemed like the best solution to get the flexibility we wanted and needed. By striking out on our own as entrepreneurs, we get to create our own rules.

I cannot imagine why men would not want the same thing—more

family time, less travel, and more skill development—but perhaps you are too afraid to ask for it. Some of you may be struggling with a different version of the same push-and-pull stresses that impact women.

But for the vast majority of you, speaking up for change in the current corporate construct would rock the boat most of you seem to so comfortably float in. Maybe you see rocking that boat as too risky? That's all I can assume as to why men have not demanded more change in their own work environments. Oh… that and the fact that their gender still puts them in the pack, and it's the pack that hunts. No girls allowed.

Men in senior leadership need to stop paying lip service to the "severe talent recruitment concern." Face it, you are not serious. Maybe you *want* to be serious, but you really aren't. Top leadership, CEOs, and boards especially repeatedly claim they are demanding—DEMANDING!—that the recruiters they hire submit a diverse roster of candidates for leadership-level job openings. And yet, if you talk one-on-one with these leaders, they will quickly follow up with, "but my choice will still be the best candidate." Translation: We are not really committed to diversity and gender inclusivity. We'll look at all the candidates and then go with what we are generally comfortable with: the candidates who look just like us. Same old, same old.

I have heard this statement far too many times from CEOs; it is their "get out of jail free card." They brag about how inclusive their recruitment practices are but then naturally fall back on what is comfortable and familiar, settling on qualities, values, and behaviors that mirror their own but which typically result in no meaningful change.

I can tell you from personal experience, no gender equity issue will ever be resolved without a bold (and I mean shout it from the rooftops), top-down initiative supported directly by the CEO and the board. The CEO must be the champion of this cause for measurable change to be achieved. And once the ball starts rolling and you have recruited some women into a few senior positions, female employees and promising future prospective female candidates will see a clear path to advancement.

Seeing women at the top makes it easier for other women to visualize their own possibilities. Without seeing women in the stereotypical senior management male roles, it's harder for women to imagine that they could hold such positions. Just look at the positive impact the *Star Trek* character of Lieutenant Nyota Uhura and the actor who portrayed her, Nichelle Nichols, had on being one of the first black women actors on a prominent US television series. Black girls who saw her character serving in a leadership capacity began to believe that maybe they, too, could go into space. As the saying goes, "If she can't see it, she can't be it." The same goes for women on boards. When an organization has more women on the board of directors, diversity will trickle down into the corporate hierarchy faster.

Additionally, there is the inertia issue, and by this, I mean the ongoing reality of men entrenched in senior positions blocking upward mobility for women. Because men are not willing to give up their coveted roles, even when it is past time, the effect amounts to lifetime employment or all the way up at the board level "'til death do us part" board seats. This means fewer senior roles for women become available. Women tend to get stuck right under that director level and cannot break through. They have two choices: leave the company or stay where they are with little chance for advancement or satisfaction.

I have witnessed many unsuccessful efforts to fix this problem, such as directing an HR department to alter its practices or by introducing a specific diversity program. Worse yet, the creation of one-off events or conferences intended to address the issue fail miserably—as if this is a one-and-done situation. Perhaps most inappropriate is passing the responsibility to the couple of women who are without significant authority in the senior ranks to effect change and then expecting they can somehow fix the situation. The solution must be driven from the top—the CEO and the board, the majority of whom are men. Once dictated from the senior-most position, the strategies necessary to succeed can be imagined, structured, and implemented. When you articulate and dictate a meaningful policy, you can also then hold your senior team accountable for the successful implementation of the new strategy. Without a well-articulated and material policy visibly supported by the top leadership, it is simply not possible to create effective and meaningful structural change in business organizations.

Women also need to be told by their employer that they are considered top talent, or a high performer, or whatever the language is in your organization. We need to end the secrecy surrounding the identification of top talent. And if women are, in fact, highly valued, an accelerated development program should be put in place for them or, if one exists, then when that female talent is identified, they should be fast-tracked into it.

It is crucial that women feel they are being invested in, being developed, so they can begin to visualize a path forward. According to the Bureau of Labor Statistics, 71.2 percent of women are working moms. Each one of those women is required to make a considerable sacrifice to balance work and family. If they do not see progress or feel that their contributions are valued, there is a good probability they are going to leave. That churn hurts the organization and impacts the culture of the organization, not to mention the bottom line.

Another reason why women are underrepresented in the leadership ranks in comparison to the number of men is that frequently women are compelled to concentrate more on the non-revenue producing side of the business, such as in legal and accounting. Whereas employees in revenue-producing roles, such as sales or marketing, are more likely to be promoted into leadership roles. Women are pretty much funneled into these non-revenue-producing roles that, once again, keep them from moving up into leadership roles. You need to stop that.

Then we have to confront the "cavemen" of an organization. These are men who will never see women as equals. They truly believe women to be lacking in the critical skills required to qualify them for leadership. More specifically, they do not see women as "deal makers." Some think that women will always be less effective than men in their decision-making, that they cannot be sufficiently objective—just not tough enough. Too emotional. Too vulnerable. They think women are weaker in leadership skills than men simply because of their gender rather than looking at the skills they bring to the table and the results they have already achieved. Some men just have blinders on, and it is unlikely we'll ever convert these cavemen to a new way of thinking.

If you are reading this and you are a caveman, it is time for you to retire and spend your days muttering, "Get your ball off my lawn!" The world has changed, is continuing to change, and you may no longer have the ability to change with it. That rigidity no longer has a place in business, or anywhere else, frankly. Not only because it is misogynistic but because it actually hurts the bottom line of the very business you are supposed to be leading—and leading into the future. The world is now too fluid and changes too quickly and too often for you to hide safely in the shallows. If I handed you my car keys and asked you to drive me to yesterday, you couldn't. Because yesterday no longer exists. Running a business from yesterday's thinking is a fool's errand and antithetical to a company's ability to succeed to its highest potential.

As to those men who are open to the idea of gender parity, we should celebrate and embolden those willing to be supportive of our ambition. Holding up positive role models can be more effective than vilifying those who will not evolve. Remember, we are looking for parity here (50 percent seems a good goal), not dominance. The idea is to partner with men in the workplace based on legitimate equality and a desire to imagine a new future. Operating out of a sense of unity and parity rather than a nervous, dysfunctional kind of counter-productive co-existence.

Recognizing Male Allies

If you want to be an ally at home, you be the one to get up in the middle of the night when your child wakes up screaming; you be the one to do the laundry or cook dinner. If you want to be an ally at work, seek out and sponsor middle management women and help them move up the ladder. Give them the credit they are due for their good work on a project or for contributing a successful idea. I have lost count of the number of times a male boss has used my ideas and taken full credit for them. Do not be that guy. Give credit where credit is due *publicly* and sponsor us in a practical and meaningful way. Your return on that investment will improve in direct proportion to the investment you make in women in senior leadership.

Be the guy who not only understands the financial business case for more women in leadership but who also understands the marketing business case. Ask, "Does the representation of women and men in senior positions at our company mirror the market served?" Understand the socio-economic business case and recognize that, by and large, if you have women who are actively present in the most senior ranks of the business, it will be better for the bottom line and employee morale, while encouraging women with potential to step up. Additionally, it is clearly better for the larger community because it recognizes a generational reality; women are in the workplace to stay.

And while we are here, let us take a moment to discuss stereotypes. We should not limit ourselves to gender-stereotypical strengths or gender-stereotypical values. Men should not automatically ascribe women attributes that are traditionally thought of as being female. Women are often brought up valuing and excelling in different skill sets that become superior leadership strengths. Women not only have the capacity to be technically brilliant at our particular jobs, but we manage the people side really well, too. Most men have to learn people skills, while most women possess these skills innately. Because of their socio/cultural upbringing, female leaders may also have developed better listening skills—something leadership coaches say men generally often need to better develop.

A new way to look at things is that what you think of, perhaps disparagingly, as female qualities are the essential elements of what are, in fact, a more well-rounded and stronger set of leadership skills than those possessed by males. Why buy a cubic zirconia when you can have a diamond?

The wrong assumptions leading to the wrong choice never makes good business sense.

Regardless of the stereotypes you were brought up to see as fact, you now have a chance to correct and update them. You must know by now that not all women are "sugar and spice and everything nice," just as men aren't made of "snips and snails and puppy dog tails." Yes, there are differences between us all, and that's exactly why it's possible to get better results when we pool our innate strengths, perspectives, and life experiences and work together as a team.

There Is No "I" in "Team"

If you really think seriously about it, leadership is about accomplishing goals through others. While there may have been a time, way back when the earth cooled, that the command-and-control style of leadership worked, it is not really an option today. It has been well-demonstrated in countless research exercises that teams make better decisions than individuals. And diverse teams make even *better* decisions.

Do you know how many team members there are on a typical Formula 1 (F1) car racing team? If you guessed fifty to seventy-five people, you'd be right. And if you include the factory and manufacturing team, it's over 1,000. Yes, it takes more than 1,000 people working in complete synchronization to get one single F1 car safely across the finish line. Yet when it comes to business, most men think they can do it all on their own.

As I mentioned earlier, when I was earning my MBA twenty-five years ago, it was all about the team. We formed teams of four and spent the next two years accomplishing our goal of earning that degree, together. We learned to communicate, present different perspectives, and persuade each other. I firmly believe that because I experienced the attitude shift over time as our team moved through the program. Having a woman on the team literally evoked a cooperative and collaborative team dynamic. I saw it, I experienced it, and I was informed by that experience throughout my career.

The need for those communications skills remains critical in terms of how the workforce is evolving. It is more diverse than ever before, which is a big advantage for teams. The younger segment of the current workforce—Gen Z, now in the early stages of their careers—have never known a world that was not team-based. Those team dynamics are second nature for them, which means that anyone who aspires to lead this generation must be cognizant of the value they place on having a voice heard in the conversation and being capable of using communication skills to engage, persuade, and motivate. As mentioned earlier, men will now have to work harder than we do to acquire these skills. You need to start exhibiting more transformational and inspirational leadership—styles associated with enhanced individual interpersonal and organizational performance, and it goes without saying, traits generally associated with women leaders.

We also need to work on men's expectations for themselves—and I am speaking about the younger men in the workforce: twenty-, thirty-, and forty-year-olds. If women are asking men to change, and if the men are saying they want to change, why has it not happened? I do not think men are lazy—I think they are under tremendous pressures of their own.

Let us reframe it from the perspective of these twenty- to forty-year-old men. More is expected of them at home, but expectations have not changed at work. Younger couples say they want (and expect) parity in their relationships, but if they cannot find relief from the pressures of work, it is not going to happen. Maybe we need to make it manly (okay, gender neutral) to spend a day with a child, or to earn less but have more family time, or to be the only father at a parent-teacher conference because your wife is traveling on business. Before the onset of the COVID pandemic, many companies had begun to offer flex policies; the trouble was men were not using them. In California and other jurisdictions, parental (bonding) leave has been initiated. However, I am willing, based on observations, to suggest that fewer than a third of men take advantage of it. What we have to do is change the corporate mindset from one where parenting is something mothers "do" to something both parents "do."

I spoke at a conference recently, and after I was done, a forty-something male approached me to let me know how much what I said resonated with him. He had a wife and two daughters and had always considered himself a solid supporter of the advancement of women in leadership. But he admitted that while listening to me speak, he realized upon reflection (to his surprise) that even though he wasn't in the "old white guys" category, his actions and his conduct exemplified behaviors I had described in the remarks and points I had made. Those attitudes were ingrained in him, but he didn't realize it until my remarks challenged him and, I hope, the rest of the attendees in the room to be more mindful.

We have recently experienced the first global pandemic in a century, one consequence of which was to force men and women to work remotely. This may have actually helped make some progress in changing the traditional gender-specific mindset.

What has changed? It is interesting to consider what the definition of "having it all" might really mean today. When I speak with women, a good third of them say that having children is not a factor in "having it all." Another third say neither is marriage. So, there are a lot of generalized misperceptions that both men and women hold about what "having it all" looks like. I think most women would define it as being satisfied that they have been able to realize self-actualization—to feel whole in their personhood, regardless of gender. It sounds to me exactly like what most men expect out of life, both at work and at play.

Women want to have the opportunity to do their best at work, to contribute, and to lead. To have that chance, men need to get their foot off the backs of our skirts, help us rise to positions of influence and power, or step out of our way. It's the only way for us all to succeed. And, like it or not, it's the future.

JUST THE FACTS, SIR.

- The percentage of Fortune 500 CEOs named John outnumbers female CEOs, the *Harvard Business Review* reported in 2018.

- According to the University of Michigan, the amount of time spent on housework varies by gender and marital status. Whether single or married, on average, women do more housework than men.

- A Furman University study found that men who requested more flexible hours were viewed more favorably than women who made the same request.

- A minority of thirty-one companies (6%) have a female CEO. In the S&P 500, there are more CEOs named James or Michael (together forty) than there are female CEOs (thirty-one) an Equileap analysis revealed in 2020.

CHAPTER 3

I'm Gonna Blow
Your Mind

OKAY, GUYS, SO THE 1920S CALLED AND THEY WANT THEIR misogyny back. Some of you have some messed-up, fossilized ideas about women in the workplace that really need to be addressed. Although we are quite capable of ignoring your outdated comments and expectations, the fact that you believe some of these crazy myths is getting in the way of our progress. That's a problem. These arcane beliefs range from "women cannot control their emotions" to "women prioritize family over work" or "women are too risk-averse to be leaders." We roll our eyes and grit our teeth when we hear this kind of nonsense because these notions serve to perpetuate stereotypes that paint women in a lesser light and call into question our ability to lead.

Even worse, these myths are patently untrue. Unfortunately, over the decades, they seem to have become accepted as fact as the uninformed among you continue to inanely repeat them. The result of having ridiculous blanket statements continually repeated is that some people start to accept them, and this then perpetually blocks women's progress upward into leadership positions.

Women Are Overlooked Leaders

Central to the problem women face is that many men do not recognize that they possess and act out of those ingrained biases. You may not realize how deeply these wrongminded stereotypes you've heard have informed how you see professional women. You may believe yourself to be totally supportive and anti-sexist, yet you will overlook or miss opportunities to bring women along.

I found myself in this very situation recently when my husband and I were dining with a friend and his wife. My friend and I were chatting away about the work I had been doing on this book and on raising awareness of the need for men to help women make more progress. I was saying that men are in the way, essentially, and need to step up to help. He was curious about that, so I explained what I had experienced and what I was trying to do to raise male awareness of the invisible barriers we face as women in the workforce, generally, and in the corporate sector, particularly.

Then, as an example, I shared the frustration surrounding finding boards of director roles I could be considered for. Boards of all sizes have been expressing a desire to become more diverse, including adding women to change the composition. However, they were not willing to simply add more positions—to increase the size of the circle so that women can participate and contribute more fully. The result is that women are being shut out, forced to wait until men step down or die before a situation exists where women could even be considered for their board positions.

Shortly after that conversation naturally wound down, my friend spoke up, addressing my husband, "Oh, Doug, before we say goodbye, I'd love to chat with you about joining my research board."

I was stunned. I like this man and greatly respect the work he does. However, come on! Not only were my credentials for the board position solid, but we had *just* finished talking about the difficulties I was experiencing in finding boards to join. I wanted to share my expertise, provide a different perspective, and introduce some positive change. Had been listening?

Although my friend had enthusiastically claimed he was a champion of women in leadership, in the next breath, he was overlooking me and asking the person at the table who looked like him to be on his board. I know he was not purposely excluding me or that he considered me to be less qualified, but the fact that he was not aware in the moment that what he was doing was excluding and dismissive was so illustrative!

The good news is that my husband declined, and soon after, I received a call from our friend apologizing for not approaching me to consider a position on his board first. Someone had pointed out his misstep, I suspect. Although I was annoyed not to be asked first, I did say yes because I truly believe I will be a valuable member of the board.

Despite my friend not immediately making the connection between his board opening and my desire to be on one, he knew my executive experience, my communication skills, and my finance background would benefit his organization. And while it did not automatically click with him that I, a woman, would be good for his board, the truth is women score higher than men in most leadership skills tests. That is not just my opinion; research published in the *Harvard Business Review* confirms it. So why do these misguided beliefs still exist at such a senior level in corporations? Perhaps simply because men want to believe them; maybe men need to believe them as part of their own male mythology. For whatever reason, they have become deeply embedded in male corporate culture.

In fact, men and women have been found to have very similar ambitions, skills, aptitudes, and attitudes. Despite this, women are treated very differently on the job, a different *Harvard Business Review* study found. "Women have less access to vital information, get less feedback from supervisors, and face other obstacles to advancement," researchers found.

In a nutshell, men are shutting women out. Through the perpetuation of this gender-biased mythology, the stereotypes hold fast and serve as a barrier for ambitious women who want to get ahead.

Myths We Need to Bust

I am sure you have heard, and maybe even believe or have repeated, many of the laughable and baseless excuses men give for why women aren't being promoted:

Women cannot control their emotions. The myth that women are incapable of controlling their emotions is utterly false. You may have trouble believing this, but it is true. You guys are allowed to be emotionally explosive, screaming and yelling at employees, and that's supposed to show great leadership (it does not, by the way). But if a woman does this, she is a bitch and out of control.

Guys, you have *no idea* how much self-control women exhibit every single day—if we did not, we would be the top story on the eleven o'clock news every night. So, yes, we actually can and do control our emotions as well as or perhaps even better than you. So, if you are looking to use this as an excuse to hold women back, keep moving. There is nothing to see here. We're not the emotional ones.

Pregnant women cannot be effective at work. We have already touched on this, but it really bears repeating. Pregnant women are no less committed to work or their employer, do not need more support, and are no less competent than their male colleagues. The idea that carrying a child suddenly negates all their skills is crazy. Do you seriously think because women bear children, they cannot possibly also be good at their jobs? I mean, seriously?! What the hell does one have to do with the other? The days of women being expected to remain barefoot and pregnant have been over for, oh, about seventy-five years.

I realize that you have no way of knowing or understanding what it is like to be pregnant, but if you strap a bowling ball onto your gut, you might get an inkling. It is uncomfortable, and it is beautiful. However, while we are growing humans inside our bodies, we women tend to receive less encouragement on the job, and, ironically, *men* whose wives are expecting tend to get more. Can you believe that?! The simple truth is women can be pregnant and effective at work at the same time. After all, we have been doing this for thousands of years. How do you think *you* got here? So, again, if you are looking for an excuse to keep us down, keep moving. This dog can't hunt either.

Now, that doesn't mean that companies don't use a pregnancy as a reason to demote or sideline women at work because they do. Elaine was at the top of her class in law school and started applying to law firms in the town where she and her husband wanted to settle. Despite being almost overqualified for any associate-level job, firms wouldn't hire her because in a few months she would suddenly be responsible for a little human—as if that totally negated her hard work and smarts. How short-sighted! And more critically, how often does this happen? Once again, the short answer: far too often.

The truth is there is a motherhood penalty that women pay, thanks to men's unwillingness to do their share. Women can have it all, but it is much easier if men are willing to step up and help out. Even when more women take on more senior roles and blaze a path forward, progress is not going to be easy. Women still do the majority of housekeeping, child-rearing, pet care, bill paying, grocery and clothes shopping, as well as staying home when children or elderly parents need them to. And if men cannot or will not step up, maybe employers need to be more creative about benefits. Rather than the standard healthcare, pension benefit, and vacation time, how about adding to the mix several hours of personal assistant/errand runner a week, childcare reimbursement, extended corporate-paid baby bonding, and the like?

Women needing and wanting support does not mean they are any less interested in or qualified for senior jobs when they become moms. I hope you are starting to see that.

Women need to emulate men to get the job done. Wrong! This is a hard "no." Just look at all the research coming out about how leaders dealt with COVID. Across the board, countries led by women had better outcomes, including the number of cases and resulting deaths. The same was found to be true of female governors in the US—that is, states with female governors had lower rates of death from COVID than states with male governors. Women own and exercise what have long been regarded by men as "less than" leadership liabilities: traits that are now demonstrably positive leadership attributes—sensitivity, perceptiveness, connectedness, and compassion. When combined with the strengths of men, the outcomes of the decisions being made collectively measurably improve. So, it is true that we do not need to emulate you because not only do we have all of your leadership skills, but we also have an arsenal of our own that makes us more effective individually and together with you collectively.

Women like pet names at work. No. Full stop. A very hard, "we will sue your ass," no! Calling women "sweetheart," "darlin'," or "honey" at work is sexist and unprofessional. It's not endearing or appreciated. Stop doing it. Using such demeaning terms is not amusing or appropriate. Contrary to what some men apparently think, women are at work to do their jobs, not to socialize or to find a husband or a baby daddy.

Don Draper was a fictional character, and best to keep it that way. Listen, if we called men pet names or played grab-ass with men at the office, we would be fired on the spot. If we cannot do it (and we certainly don't want to), neither can you. Knock it off. We are professionals just like you, here to do our jobs and go home. Get over yourselves

The way we dress indicates interest in a relationship. False. We dress for ourselves, just like you do. No matter how we dress, keep your hands to yourself. (#MeToo) Sexual harassment continues to run rampant through organizations of all sizes and industries. A survey from the Pew Research Center found that 69 percent of women who had been sexually harassed had it happen in a professional or work setting. Yet only a small number of women who have been sexually harassed ever file a formal report because they fear retaliation. Turns out their fear is justified.

I do not dress for you. I dress for me. As a grown-up, it is your responsibility, not mine, to keep your adolescent hormones in check. And please do not give me the BS about how men cannot help it, that it is nature at work. You are an adult. Yes, you can behave like an adult. You have to. It is not a request. Just do it and move on. Again, as I said above, don't flatter yourself.

Women are not as educated. Yet another major false assumption made by far too many men. More women have been earning high school diplomas, associate degrees, bachelor's degrees, and master's degrees than men for some time now. Like it or not, overall, women are actually better educated than men.

I do not know what else to say about this one except the truth is the truth. So, thinking that you are smarter than the women in your office only proves the point that we are better educated than you. Think about that.

Speaking softly is a sign of weakness or incompetence. Once again, so preposterously wrong. Women can speak softly and still carry a big stick. We may not be as physically large as you, but given the aforementioned advanced degrees, we can often find solutions to a situation or problem that men have not thought of. *Harvard Business Review* confirms this, reporting that women score higher on IQ, emotional intelligence, creativity, and leadership skills tests. In addition, "women account for at least 50 percent of the most talented part of the workforce." Translation: Women represent at least half of the most talented employees in corporate settings. We are not the weakest link. Just stop and think for a moment. Combined, the efforts of women and men working cooperatively toward a common purpose invariably improve the probability of better corporate outcomes. Magical thinking? No, just well-established gender corporate reality. Read the research.

Nor are we on the gridiron when we are in the office, guys. We do not need to scream and shout and be aggressive like a coach with his varsity team. You have no idea how ridiculous you all look when you are doing your "man things." You also have no idea how difficult it is to keep from rolling our eyes every time you guys want to wrestle or measure your package sizes or whatever it is you do to prove dominance. We are here to do a job, and that does NOT require aggression or screaming. Got it? Okay then.

Misperceptions about Women

Despite all of the research that backs up positive statements about women and their capabilities, you men do not seem to want to hear it. Or maybe, as I said earlier, you do not want to believe it because it puts your jobs at risk. So, you go out of your way to convince others—both men and women—that women are less capable at work, saddled with home obligations that supersede their job responsibilities, and that they are not truly interested in leadership roles for those reasons.

Oh, *really*? I think it is much more likely that in the last fifty or sixty years, men have concocted this notion to make themselves feel better when they take steps to keep women down.

In fact, a number of American cultural norms signal that women should not pursue leadership roles. Culturally, women have been conditioned to take a back seat or to prioritize family over ambition at work, not because they lack capability, education, ambition, or capacity but because their subservience makes life easier for you. Think about this statement. These cultural norms include:

Different expectations for women and men. Men are expected to be providers, while women are expected to play a supporting role. Being a good mother is also celebrated more than being a good professional. Those expectations are then translated into fewer career opportunities.

Early exposure to rigid gender roles/norms. While you are taught and expected to "take charge," women are expected to "take care." Caretaker roles are almost always assigned to women, as are office housekeeping tasks, by default.

Devalued societal notion of a "balanced" life. Men whose lives are dominated by work are respected more than women who choose to work in the home as moms. We are all taught that it is nearly inconceivable that professional, personal, and social lives could be integrated. Which is why women get stuck in caregiver roles while you men continue working late nights to get ahead at work. Neither of these terms has a place in today's social economy.

Lack of support for each other. We are taught that women (and men) will negatively judge other women who make different work or family choices, even though today's economic reality virtually dictates the need for dual-income households. Words like "catty" are used, suggesting that women are a lot like forever-feuding Alexis and Krystle on the soap opera *Dynasty*, when the reality is they are more like friends Carrie, Miranda, and Charlotte on *Sex and the City*.

But this last point, especially, seems like just another convenient excuse—that other women are to blame for the lack of progress in the advancement of women rather than the men who are in positions of power.

Female bosses can get a bad rap for being harder on the women who work for them than male managers are. While there are certainly some women (just as there are some men) whose ambition overrides all else, the vast majority of women I have encountered are generous, encouraging, and committed to helping other women succeed—to pulling them up the career ladder. A quote from Madeleine Albright, the first female US secretary of state—"There's a special place in hell for women who don't help other women"—really resonates with me.

Women, more than men, fear taking risks or attempting new challenges unless there is a real probability of success. No. More often, women are just more thoughtful in their analysis, caring about how a business risk should be addressed, how it will affect people, and the probability of a successful outcome of the strategy intended to overcome the challenge. We are thinking, we are analyzing, and then strategizing, and all the while, we are learning. And we do not feel the need to loudly and repeatedly comment on everything. Do not take our silence during a meeting as a sign of indifference to the matter at hand, a lack of comprehension of the issue, technical incompetence, or emotional immaturity.

We participate differently but generally with better outcomes than you men achieve. Imagine that.

Women want to be liked more than we want power. Seriously, that is another hard "no." While that may be true for some women, it is more likely to be true for men because, for men in business, you either ingratiate, dominate, or become deliberately invisible as you scheme and dream your way forward. As a gender, whether they are liked or not does not impact or influence women's decision-making abilities.

Women are not interested in senior leadership roles. Really? Put yourself in the shoes of the women in your life and think about that statement or, better yet, ask them the question. Why would women *not* be interested in being promoted? Gender has nothing to do with interest in or qualification for more senior executive roles and responsibilities. Stop leaning on that assumption to rationalize not offering women opportunities to progress within your organization. Assume the obvious! Of course, they want advancement.

Women's "feminine" leadership qualities are not as important or as relevant and are not valued as much as men's. A single statement with all three elements wrong. The statement is quantifiably, qualifiedly, and statistically dead wrong. The male notion of the relative value of "street" male and female leadership qualities is deeply ingrained in male corporate culture—the culture men invented—and that notion is punishingly wrong. We do not need women behaving as men. We need women managing and leading as women.

The business world today is more about being able to understand ever-changing markets, consumer psychographics, connectivity, collaboration, empathy, and a deep cultural awareness within the business organization in terms of how to get the best work out of every employee—all of which abilities are at the heart of female sensibility. It seems it is clear to everyone but you that you may need to change your suppositions about leadership qualities. It's very clear that we collectively need to change something here structurally.

What if men could be taught to think more like women? How about men get some form of institutional training to better help them understand and incorporate some feminine leadership attributes into their management perspective? Consider that kind of paradigm shift rather than the same old, same old, with women being compelled to learn and adopt "male traits" for the purpose of making them more male-like in their leadership behavior. Remember, women leaders have higher overall bottom-line success rates than you do!

Board positions are men's domain. If I had a dollar for every time a man described his board, comprised of a dozen or more individuals, two of whom are women, as "diverse," I would be a very rich woman. Unfortunately, an embarrassingly small number of large corporate boards are truly diverse. A truly diverse board would be comprised of 50 percent female, 50 percent male, racially and ethnically blended so it more broadly represented the market served, rather than today's composition of a token woman or two, while keeping an eye on a balance of other candidate attributes.

There is a direct correlation between the number of women on boards and the number of women who are part of the most senior executive teams—which probably explains our current situation. The more leaders move women into executive roles, the more opportunities they will have to ascend to corporate board positions. To do that, leaders could and should encourage female and male board members to establish relationships with future women leaders and to serve as role models, mentors, or sponsors for board positions. They could, and they should, but they don't. And this book is about why they won't and why that has to change. Now.

Here is what private and public companies miss out on. You may be shocked to learn that women-led companies on the S&P 500 consistently outperform the male-led firms. The thirty-two companies with women CEOs "have significantly outperformed the companies run by men. Over the past ten years, the difference in returns is 384 percent from female-led companies vs. 261 percent from male-led companies," reports Personal Finance Club on Instagram, which ran the comparison.

Give Women the Chance They Deserve

Female directors accelerate progress on gender diversity. However, if male directors do not wish to "get out of the way to make room for gender parity" at the board table, how about opening positions or expanding the board's size? As an example, I was recently speaking with a good friend who sits on the board of a very large multinational corporation. His perspective was that even expanding a board to add women would not really achieve much in that the women's voices are still diluted at the board table. I strongly disagree. Women's voices, even in few numbers, will bring a perspective that is currently absent. In addition, their mere presence will demonstrate to board members their capability and to other women that there is indeed a place for them and the possibility of a future at the highest levels of the organization.

Or how about committing to replacing the next three or four open board positions with qualified women as a major step toward gender parity? At a minimum, at least commit to holding firm on the number of board positions women currently occupy so that we cannot be driven backward, further away from full gender parity.

Recently, another good friend of mine stepped down from an industry association board due to her changing jobs, which then presented a conflict of interest. She had been one of eight women on a twenty-four-person board. As she planned her leave, she thought it important (and responsible) to find a replacement candidate to represent her constituency—a woman. She called a half dozen women she knew who could shine in the position and was successful in finding the perfect candidate. The organization's governance rules called for an emergency election, so she did her best to give her candidate all the guidance and advice on how to announce her candidacy early so that others might be discouraged by a contest. She also spent time socializing her candidacy and campaigning for her. It seemed that her plan stood a pretty good chance of working.

However, a couple of weeks before the election, a male candidate made it known that he would run against her. He was well known to the constituency, so he had a significant advantage in that regard. It should have been apparent to him from the source of the candidate's sponsorship that he should withdraw his candidacy and make it understood that he did so to provide support to the female candidate. He was a very highly regarded senior executive in her industry. So, one would think he might have asked himself how he wanted his legacy to read. That he put in three years on this prestigious board or that he deliberately and publicly withdrew his candidacy because it was the right thing to do—to lift up and showcase a very qualified woman who he knew to be a stellar candidate?

His action would not have increased the number of women on that board by stepping aside. It would simply have kept the number of women board members at the status quo. But what an opportunity he had to shape the future of the board, to maintain the hard-won gender platform that could continue creating board gender parity, all by simply withdrawing his candidacy. Further, he could have demonstrated to his male cronies that attitudinal change could be made by a senior male leading the way, showing his male counterparts how it could be done, in the hopes that they would learn from him and follow suit, not just in relation to the outcome on this particular board but rather in the general direction of broader corporate gender parity.

So, you are no doubt asking yourself—what did he do in the face of this opportunity to get it right? Well, he chose to continue his run at the board position, clearly signaling that he had no intention or interest in standing down or aside on the basis of gender parity. Implicitly, he was also sending the message that, in spite of her very obvious but less well-known qualifications as a candidate, she was not yet ready to occupy this board position. She soldiered on as a determined woman of principle, believing in the need for women to step into the virtual breach of the ongoing gender struggle faced by women.

The election was held and he won the seat, which was not surprising since there were a lot more men than women on that voting roster. What was most disappointing was the clear message received by all (board, management, and employees) that diversity was not valued by the constituents in this organization. It became quite apparent that despite plenty of DEI investments, none of the constituents, the organization, or its board or committees had any real plans to include women in its senior-most ranks at the board level.

DEI 101

For anyone who may not yet be familiar with the concept of DEI (diversity, equity, and inclusion), these are initiatives specifically designed to make organizations fairer in terms of who has a say in how they are run. In a nutshell, diversity is where every American is invited to register to vote, regardless of gender, race, ethnicity, or sexual orientation. Equity is when every vote counts the same (one person, one vote). And inclusion is that all votes are counted to determine the winner and the course of our country.

In a business sense, at a senior management level, diversity is all about hiring and engaging people who are not just different on the outside but who also bring a different perspective to the workplace because of their gender, race, cultural backgrounds, and varied life experiences. These differences can add an "out-of-the-box" perspective to problem-solving and add new ways to grow the business, not the least of which may be expanding our existing concept of markets by recognizing the criticality of inclusiveness.

Equity is about giving these differing perspectives honest consideration, no matter where in the senior ranks of the organization chart they originated.

Inclusion is about giving everyone responsible for the consequences of an outcome a seat at the actual decision-making table where they can make a real impact on the success of the business enterprise.

Although we have been hearing a lot of noise about DEI from organizations of all sizes, in fact, a great number of companies are scrambling to put a DEI policy and program in place. More important, however, is that most male-dominated C-suite executives are not convinced that DEI is a significant issue within *their* companies.

This is where I get a little confused. By refusing to acknowledge it as an issue, the situation is perpetuated so that even today, it is very clear there are far too few women in leadership roles in large corporations—that is a fact. Yet, all, and I do mean all, of the data either establishes, indicates, or suggests that having women in senior decision-making roles is unequivocally good for business. When women are involved, companies make more money, are more efficient (lower churn), and are able to attract a better, broader talent pool.

So, why do men invest so much energy in keeping women down, if not out, obstructing the efforts to make DEI progress? If you think it's not happening in your company, there is a simple way to double-check your math: Count. Take a headcount and determine how many women your company has in the most senior management positions, in senior director positions, in the C-suite, and what the makeup is of your board of directors. Numbers don't lie. Once you have your numbers, take step #2: Actually ask your employees how they feel about that. Like any good business decision you make, do the research. You might be surprised that your company is not as far along with DEI compliance as you thought. Once you know the facts, you won't be able to pretend there isn't a problem, or you can, but it is on you and—know this—you will be called out.

Pushing for DEI Progress

If you are an employee and curious to learn if your employer is serious about including and advancing women in decision-making and interested in fostering their involvement in more senior management positions, why not investigate? Ask questions about the number of women in senior roles, the percentage of women who have recently been promoted out of those who are eligible, and about your company's strategies and programs in place or plans to advance women within the organization. Ask about mentorship programs, ask about continued education or specialized training that might be available within the company; ask HR to provide access to the DEI reports for the last few years. If your employer is truly serious, HR must be developing or already have a well-developed implementation plan, right?

As an employer, once you have a clearer view of where your company stands, you need to expand your circle of influencers to include those who see DEI as an issue to be addressed in the company. What is their perspective, even if it is different from your own? As the "boss," engage with every level of employee to get their perspective on DEI within the company. Consider making the inquiries anonymous to get an honest evaluation of how you, as a company and as an executive, are doing with DEI.

And outside your company, speak with other executives who have begun to approach the issue in their organizations. The next time you are at a business gathering, spend time discussing this subject with your fellow leaders. It does not matter who gets it right first so long as someone gets it and shares the answer. You can go back to speaking about the lesser issues, including purely social conversation, when you are done, but be absolutely resolute and deliberate in your inquiries about who is doing what, how they are doing it, and what outcomes they are realizing in the movement to fully embrace DEI.

When I have spoken with male senior executives about DEI, what I have heard is that they are fearful of making the wrong decisions about implementing a program. Doing nothing on that basis is easy to rationalize. But know this, not for a moment do we buy it. You routinely make million-dollar decisions, but you want women to believe you cannot muster the intellectual energy for the focused consideration required to understand the critical importance of DEI. Seriously? And that is why corporations usually only confront the subject when they are compelled to, when they are in crisis, even knowing, as they most assuredly do, that crisis management is antithetical to thoughtful planning. Acknowledge, address, research, plan, program, and start implementation. You may be in the majority who have not begun this process. Best to start yesterday.

Senior executives are always looking for results—more sales, more clients, lower costs, and more profitability. The trouble is that DEI results look a lot different and do not initially or directly reflect their impact. However, over time the impact on net income may be significantly beyond expectations. Through DEI, you will see more engaged employees, less costly employee churn and better collaboration, and a better talent pool, all of which typically drive long-term profitability.

The key is patience. The issue of DEI has been systemically ignored for decades, so do not expect overnight results. You *can* expect a lot of feedback, which will likely feel like pushback from your male executives and managers. But you are going to have to view it as *push forward*. And yes, a lot of time and energy will be invested that may not appear to be producing measurable results or affecting the bottom line for some time as the issue is being addressed. You have to establish both short- and long-term strategies and goals and be prepared to celebrate the wins along the way.

To be successful, you will need to be corporately "all in" and totally committed. Very importantly, stop viewing DEI as a side issue—it is a business issue that, unaddressed, is negatively affecting your business as you read this, and continued inattention will negatively impact your business for years to come.

It is the twenty-first century, and you need to recognize what the real rolled-up and projected cost of clinging to these mistaken assumptions, beliefs, and outright myths about women in the workplace has been and continues to be. If you are able and willing to "get with the program" and let go of gender stereotypes, imagine the change from within you can affect.

No matter if you are a CEO or an accounting manager, every day you have the opportunity to support, empower and elevate women working around you. You can do that by showing appreciation, making an intro-duction, championing some bright young woman, sharing an insight or resource, or encouraging others to see in themselves the possibilities, po-tential, and opportunities they might not see otherwise. Every time you do, you demonstrate the very sort of leadership the world is so hungry to see. Compassionate leadership. Courageous leadership. Humane leadership. Leadership qualities that are not, and have never been, as prevalent in the men who dominate corporations.

Your knee-jerk reaction to this might be, "Listen, I don't have time to handhold my employees or stroke their egos. I have work to do." I earnestly suggest that this may be the most important work you might have before you. You need to believe that showing genuine appreciation and demon-strating meaningful inclusivity IS a guaranteed way of increasing your company's bottom line. Personnel turnover is costly, as is employee apathy and the silent bitterness and frustration that gets in the way of committed productivity and often ends in *quiet quitting*. It is a smart business decision that just so happens to be the right thing to do. Win and win.

JUST THE FACTS, SIR.

- Women got higher performance ratings than men but were con-sistently—and incorrectly—judged as having less leadership po-tential in a study by Professor Kelly Shue, which was reported in a Yale School of Management article.

- Women leaders are most likely to embody "compassionate wis-dom," which is "the leadership style most likely to drive engaged, happy, and productive teams, reducing the negative human capital costs companies fear today," *Fast Company* reported.

- Men misperceive a desire for work and family balance as hold-ing women back. A survey conducted at Stanford and reported in *Harvard Business Review* found that "The men in our survey

60

largely attributed gender disparities to individual choice. For instance, when asked what holds women back from senior leadership positions, the most common response from men was women's desire to balance work and family. Women, in contrast, said the biggest barriers to advancement are systemic factors like stereotyping and exclusion from networks of communication and influence."

- Sexual harassment training may not actually help reduce its occurrence, *Harvard Business Review* found. In fact, training made men more likely to blame the victim.

CHAPTER 4

You Help Us and We'll Help You – Make More Money

O F COURSE, MEN MATTER IN THE CORPORATE WORLD. YOU matter. I am not suggesting otherwise or downplaying how important you are to the corporate construct. In fact, you are essential to everyone's success, primarily because, at the moment, you are the critical catalyst capable of propelling women upward in corporate America. Without your support, that movement of women into the upper echelons of corporate power won't happen. Or it might, but it could get very messy.

More importantly, the economy needs you to step up—now—to drive the effort to get more women into positions of power, and you know why. I will say it yet again: When you let us in, we *all* make more money, our businesses are more strongly positioned in the marketplace, and we produce better, more targeted products and services for our clients and customers. It is a simple, and to repeat it again, well-established fact.

Before I show you the "how" and "why," I think we must address the elephant in the room, which is the very apparent reluctance of men in senior positions to help.

I know you have been hesitating, and I can only assume that is because you think pulling women up beside you or near you will put you at a disadvantage of some sort. So, let us talk about why that is simply not true.

Helping women get ahead is good for you and for us. As I said earlier, it is a very predictable win/win for everyone—financially, socioeconomically, and emotionally.

Let us look at just some of the ways having women involved in decision-making has been proven to reap big rewards. More women in leadership positions creates:

- **More innovation.** Adding more women to the management ranks increased revenue from innovation by 2.5 percent, Boston Consulting Group (BCG) found, and adding them to IT teams increased patent citations by 26 to 42 percent, UC Berkeley research found. Women think differently than you. Not better or worse, just differently. And that different point of view can take your business from good to great or from struggling to viable and from viable to thriving. Innovation keeps businesses competitive both now and in the future. Without innovation, businesses die. Women help businesses survive and thrive.

- **Improved financial metrics.** Companies with more "gender diverse leadership" achieved higher returns on capital, higher margins, and lower volatility, according to Credit Suisse. Not only that but "the best-performing companies in terms of share price display superior diversity in both the boardroom and the C-suite," said that same report. Again, if you want to make more money, you have to make a place for us in the boardroom and equally, and just as importantly, in the C-suite.

- **More sales.** Companies with more gender-diverse boards had a 42 percent higher return on sales, 66 percent higher return on invested capital, and a 53 percent higher return on equity, Duke University summarized in a Catalyst study. Read that sentence again and let it really sink in. You'll make more money.

- **Higher share price.** Companies with more than 20 percent management diversity—meaning more women—have traded at an average premium of 13 percent versus companies with less than

15 percent female representation in management. Said another way, according to a Credit Suisse exec, "The higher the female representation across the companies we cover, the better share price returns we have observed since 2010." More women mean increased share value. Are you seeing a pattern here?

- **Better credit ratings.** Corporate boards with greater gender diversity have better credit quality, Moody's found. We know that, generally speaking, better credit quality means greater borrowing capacity and a lower cost of money.

- **More worker talent.** The more diverse a workforce, the more attractive the organization is to new hires. Eighty-five percent of female millennials consider workplace diversity and company policies on inclusion when choosing an employer, PwC reported. Nobody works effectively forever, and at some point, you are going to have to replenish your leadership. Why not start now and start moving your female superstars into leadership positions. To get the best of the best, you are going to need to show these female up-and-comers that you know and appreciate their value to the company and that you will have their backs and are cognizant of their expectations for their future advancement. Always remember, you need them as much and, possibly, more than they need you.

- **Positive corporate culture.** A positive relationship was reported between gender diversity and organizational cultures that highly value teamwork, participation, and cohesiveness, the National Center for Women and Information Technology reported. Not only that but gender diversity is highly correlated with workplace happiness. More women around makes for happier employees. We are not window-dressing, believe it or not. We are a valuable asset to every company. Women in leadership roles create an environment where more desirable outcomes are probable. Have I said that too often? I think not.

- **More controversy.** Companies with corporate boards that lacked diversity generally had "more governance-related controversies" than those with more women involved in corporate oversight, MSCI discovered. Meaning companies are more likely to get in trouble. Fewer women on boards means a greater chance of ethics violations, conflicts of interest, a lack of oversight or protection of shareholder interests, accountability problems, and a lack of transparency—all of which can result in costly lawsuits, penalties, and fines. Let us help keep you out of trouble.

- **Lower collective intelligence.** Companies with a greater proportion of women in senior management "was associated with higher collective intelligence." Meaning the intelligence level of the company as a whole (its corporate IQ) is higher with more women present in the ranks of senior management. Translation: Companies with a majority of men in senior management were, therefore, corporately less intelligent overall. Hey, the facts are the facts. What can we say? Collective intelligence is important for better problem-solving, strategizing, and decision-making. So, the more women involved, the better your results.

- **Worse decisions.** All-male teams make better decisions than individuals alone 58 percent of the time, but gender-diverse teams blow that number out of the water, outperforming individual decision makers 73 percent of the time. Men alone get the worst results. I know those two statements might sting a little, but by increasing the number of women senior managers (to 50 percent, *at least*, and not just by a token woman or two!), many of a business organization's serious problems can be resolved more readily and with fewer significant negative consequences for the organization.

I am not surprised by any of this information. These are just a few examples of how women help companies achieve better results than men can alone. We both know there are many more.

So, what is stopping you from helping us make more progress? You know that leaving us out of your organization puts you at a competitive disadvantage, so why the reluctance? Why the foot dragging? Seriously, I want to understand because it doesn't make sense to me why you continue to exclude us.

We need men engaged in the solution. I am sure you have women in your lives who are impacted by this; maybe you have a young daughter and knowing what you know about corporate environment, you worry for her future. Men typically want everything for their daughters that they want for their sons—a chance for them to be all they can be, to accomplish all they are capable of. Men do not want the women in their lives to be debased, sidelined, held back, or prevented from succeeding simply because of their gender. So, why isn't that mindset taken to the office every day? By you.

When you are at work, we need you to advocate for us. Men have the power and women just want our share of it. We are not trying to take over, only asking to be treated like we make a difference because you know we do. And even if you didn't know, you certainly do now. Nowhere to hide.

I have said before, I am talking about an easily rationalized, equal power split. Adding one or two women into leadership roles is great, but you need to hit critical mass of 50 percent of us being in leadership roles to make this work to its fullest potential—otherwise, you are just wasting your time and our skills. Think of it this way. For every ten percent you fall short of that 50 percent, you are leaving a potential 10 percent of available but unrealized income on the table. Do you really want to do that? Or worse, be seen to be knowingly doing that by your board, your shareholders, or your employees? I would hope not.

Speaking of wasting skills, my friend Deirdre started her career in the marketing department of a Fortune 500 company. She was promoted at least once a year, reaching director level quickly, but because she was in her twenties, no one took her seriously when it came to strategizing. No matter that she was one of only three people in her department with a specialized

MBA, the senior executives seemed to feel she lacked the experience that would qualify her to have an opinion on important topics.

The company began work to develop a product that, based on Deirdre's analysis, no one wanted or needed. Deirdre spoke out to almost anyone who would listen, expressing reservations about all the resources being sunk into what she thought was a dud of a product. However, the excitement level around this new product introduction internally reached a fever pitch, drowning out any constructive criticism Deirdre and others offered.

She left soon after the product was launched, taking a job at a company that valued her expertise. In less than ten years, the new product was scrapped as the company fought to stay relevant after its major misstep, ultimately declaring bankruptcy. Until the very end, the company had resisted promoting women into its senior ranks, and those who were didn't stay for long. Harsh way to learn the hard reality of the cost of excluding talented women from your ranks.

We are talking to you because we do not really have to convince women that their involvement is a good idea. They get it. They live with the issues and challenges faced by Deirdre every day, and they know that things would be different, would be better, if they had a hand in some of the decision-making that goes on around them. We can (and do!) talk about this amongst ourselves *ad nauseam* and have been trying to get your attention focused on this subject for decades—unsuccessfully, of course. Until you proactively help us in quantifiable ways to reach the boardrooms and C-suites, your companies will suffer and so will your stockholders.

Researching the Problem

Because I truly want to understand where men are coming from with respect to women in the workplace and why it's been almost impossible to make any kind of significant progress toward women's advancement into senior-level jobs, I commissioned my own research study. My thinking was that the only way to turn the tide is to get into the heads of male employees and grasp why they won't help women progress. I wanted to understand how employees view women at work and their prospects for leadership. So, in March 2022, I surveyed 260 adults over the age of twenty-five in the US who were employed full-time and earning at least $75,000. About half were men and half were women.

I expected the results to be clear and convincing, to shed light on what the specific roadblocks are and what men and women think we should do about it. They were anything but. In fact, there were no major differences or discernable patterns based on gender throughout the responses. Meaning both men and women have bought into some of the stereotypes that have permeated our culture. Both men and women are in the way of women's advancement. Unsurprisingly it would seem that women have come to expect inferior treatment, and men have an ingrained sense of entitlement that is difficult to relinquish.

There were also some commonalities, however.

When asked about desirable characteristics for corporate leaders, 80.4 percent responded "effective communicator," 44.6 percent said "respect for others," 37.7 percent said "actively listens," 36.5 percent said "skilled problem-solver," and 35 percent said "takes personal responsibility." Perhaps surprisingly, given what we hear about what makes a leader, is that only 12.7 percent listed "charisma" and 12.3 percent listed "stays current on industry trends"—both at the bottom of the list. The takeaway here is that there is no consensus on the characteristics a corporate leader should have other than effective communication.

Female Entitlement

Lest you happen to think that women are asking for too much here, I can assure you that you are wrong. Dead wrong. In fact, women consistently ask for *less* than they deserve, almost across the board. They rarely push for what they merit, even when witnessing less qualified men getting more. You need to wonder what type of working environment encourages, insists, or imposes this literal devaluation of the relative worth of a woman's contribution to the success of the company.

There is a women's entitlement problem at play in the corporate world. A study done by Cornell University, where men and women were asked to determine pay rates they considered fair for certain labor, was particularly alarming. Men suggested pay valued at 63 percent more than women. Women's and men's expectations for pay rates differ tremendously, which helps explain why we have such pay inequity. Women continue to undervalue their work, while men, conversely, continue to overvalue theirs. This should shock and appall you. Like Patty Hearst and the SLA, we've been living our own Stockholm syndrome life for decades. Congratulations, gentlemen! You undervalue women in the workplace, and we believe you. Now, we're all losing money because of that. Fantastic. Damn, you are clever!

Additionally, the same study asked each gender to work on a task until they felt they had earned a certain fixed pay rate. Women worked 22 percent longer than men and accomplished 32 percent more of the task. After learning this, you might think that women would be resentful at having had to work longer and faster to earn what it took men less time to earn. But no, shockingly, the men and women were equally satisfied with their pay. Again, this should really keep you awake at night. *Really* think about what that means. Somebody is getting a free ride, and it ain't the girls!

Women tend to accept what they are offered, while men ask for more. That has to change. We need your support and encouragement to feel confident in asking for more (i.e., what we're worth), as well as your agreement not to put roadblocks in our way when we DO ask for more. You know that our work is worth just as much as a man's, and the research above suggests that we may well be more productive than men for the same compensation. So how about acknowledging that and then advocating for us to get us the pay we deserve instead of taking shameless advantage of what I refer to as the "female discount."

Speaking of this "female discount," I recently reconnected with a long-time friend of mine who caught me up on what was happening in her work life. I had followed her career for over three decades. She was all in, kind of a lifer in each of the two companies she worked for over those decades. She raised a family while taking on ever-increasing roles and responsibilities. She advanced up the corporate ladder as an internal candidate for every promotion. After ten years at the second of her employers, her boss retired. She felt ready, and she jumped at the chance to apply to fill this role—an executive position reporting directly to the CEO and at a pay rate at least 25 percent more than she was currently making.

She had paid her dues. She had all the experience, bona fides, credentials, a solid knowledge of the people, and she understood the working dynamics of the company. She was well respected by fellow employees through all levels of management, at the board level, and was known to many of the company's customers. This was her big chance.

She gave it her best shot and heard later that she stood out in the interview process against very qualified external candidates. Human resources called her to congratulate her on being selected for the new executive position. They also told her that she would be receiving an increase in her pay—a full 8 percent increase—which HR explained was the maximum awarded to anyone receiving an internal promotion. Although pleased to receive the promotion, she was very disappointed with the salary proposed and told HR so. She pressed for an explanation as to why, given that she would be doing the same job as the man who had just retired from the position, she wasn't going to be compensated at the same pay rate—a rate, she added, that would have been offered to attract an external candidate, male or female. HR stuck to the offer of an 8 percent pay raise, rationalizing that increase as "policy." Take it or leave it.

So, my friend arranged to speak directly with the CEO. He was quick to respond to her, repeating what she had heard from HR about the "policy" with respect to internal hires, but said he was open to reviewing the situation with HR. HR let him know that he might have to increase the pay rate as it was possible that my friend would be raising the situation as a "diversity" issue.

This was not a diversity issue. If the company had selected an external candidate, male or female, it would have had to pay the market rate—the rate my friend was asking for. What this clearly represented was a situation where the company was trying to realize on a captive "female discount." Call it whatever you want, the best candidate, a woman in this case, was about to be taken advantage of once again by being offered less than what the man who had previously held the position was making.

This is precisely how capable, qualified women are often treated inequitably, even as they move into senior posts in their quest for an opportunity to join the executive pipeline. Women are still a bargain, but pay them what they are worth and then realize the additional value for the same money you are paying your male employees.

This story does have a happy ending in that my friend not only got the position but received the pay scale she had fought for. Kudos to the CEO who was willing to reconsider and overturn a historic but arbitrary company policy.

This could have ended as just another typical classic example of an absence of gender mindfulness. Had the CEO not been prepared to revisit the policy and simply assumed HR would handle the outcome in an equitable manner, the company would doubtless have lost a key experienced senior executive.

And to the women reading this—you need to know your value and fight for the promotions you believe you are qualified and ready for. Don't just be grateful for the job you have; you already deserve that one. What's next? Expect more, ask for more, insist on more! And, please, don't expect HR to manage and elevate you in your career. They generally manage using the rules in place—rules typically created by male senior managers. If you are not getting the response you want and believe you deserve, don't hesitate to go straight to the source to fight for appropriate compensation.

As was shared with you earlier, major peer-reviewed research has shown time and again that gender-diverse companies perform better than entirely homogeneous ones, or at least male-dominated ones. Unfortunately, even when presented with the unimpeachable evidence derived from countless research studies, male-dominated companies do not want to change course. Men who run companies—public, private, or non-profit—like things just the way they are. It is almost as if you guys are afraid of having the proverbial curtain pulled back and being revealed as Oscar Diggs instead of the Great and Powerful Oz.

I will let you in on a little secret: Women already know what men in the corporate world have been up to for decades. We know you must be aware that we know this. We also know you are aware and, for whatever reason, turn a blind eye to the fact that your organizations aren't performing optimally, that they could be better.

This exposes another significant impact of the unresolved gender parity problem. It's a problem for the corporations generally, public or private. Companies underperforming and not realizing their full fiscal potential is bad for the economy at large. It's bad for shareholders, bad for the general public when the larger economy underperforms as a result. Really, when is it ever good to settle for lesser results than you could have achieved?!

The Good News about Women Leaders

We understand that men would rather be in charge than cede that role to women. The same goes for women. That proclivity is not an issue of gender. But what men need to understand and accept is that, sometimes, a particular woman is the better choice for a job.

Xerox Corporation is a case in point. Ursula Burns, who rose through the ranks of Xerox from college intern to its first Black woman CEO, was responsible for pulling the company back from the brink when she took the helm in 2009; she remained as the company's CEO until 2016 when it was split into two companies.

After landing a college internship in 1980, Burns was quickly tagged as an up-and-coming leader by men and women alike within the company for her brutal honesty and intelligence, *Fast Company* details. She spoke up when others did not, soon catching the eye of several key executives who moved her into executive assistant roles early in her career where she could shadow top executives. While she was rising in the ranks, Xerox, the company, was on a steep downslide. *Fast Company* called Xerox at that time "a dying company," competing in the face of very strong Japanese companies emerging globally in the photocopy space and with the onslaught of digital technology.

However, Anne Mulcahy, a Xerox sales exec, and Burns seemed to be moving up the career ladder in tandem. So, when Mulcahy was named CEO in 2000, she tapped Burns to take over the enormous task of outsourcing the company's manufacturing. Xerox had to in order to survive. As the vice president of worldwide manufacturing, not only did Burns get Xerox's union to agree to the outsourcing, which was a feat in itself, but she also led the company's foray into color copying. From near bankruptcy in 2000, Xerox was once again profitable by 2004.

Immediately after being named CEO in 2009, succeeding Mulcahy, when Xerox's market capitalization was $7.35 billion, Burns took steps to push the company in a new direction—into the massive business services market, which she estimated to be worth $500 billion. Her challenge was evolving "The Document Company" to a business process outsourcing company at a time when analysts were unsure that was the right play.

When Burns stepped down in 2016 and the company was split into two entities, Conduent (worth $7 billion) and the new Xerox (worth $11 billion), she had already succeeded in entering new markets, acquiring pivotal companies, and setting a course forward for the company.

Could a man have done as well? Most folks at Xerox don't think so, and still don't.

Some of you may argue that, yes, a man would have taken a different tack, made different decisions, and approached their role as leader differently. But many observers, inside and out, believe that she was what the company had needed in the moment. She had an engineering background, decades of experience within the company, and a commitment to brutal honesty that many within the company respected and an honesty not enough executives at the company practiced.

Her ability to look at the company and the market through a different, and female, lens is what made her, and Xerox, successful.

Understanding What Women Bring to the Table

If you are skeptical that Burns did a better job than a man could have, do not forget that her predecessor, Anne Mulcahy, took over from a male CEO who only lasted thirteen months before giving up. Women are different in ways that men do not entirely understand.

As I see it, there are four things men need to know about the women they work with, facts that they probably are not aware of:

1) Women already know and have pretty much accepted that life is not always fair. We get it, and we have for a long time. Many men like things just the way they are. That does not mean we will give up looking for ways to make progress. We may have realized that we women are unlikely to be able to force change from within, but it is perhaps clearer than ever that men at the top of senior management, both within the corporation and at the board level, certainly can if they choose to.

The question I wish more men would ask themselves is, "What can I do to help level the uneven playing field for women?" Which means actually *doing* something when women ask you for help and feedback. Help us continue to learn and grow so that we can help you win, too. And do NOT give our male peers an undeserved gender advantage.

Most of all, when we speak up about inequity or parity, for God's sake, LISTEN and HELP! TAKE ACTION! Do not just pat us on the head and express concern about our sorry state as if there was nothing you could do to alter that sorry state. Because there is! And if you are not prepared to really step up and effect change, then at the very least give credit where credit is due. Acknowledge what our real contribution is. That would matter a lot. Don't steal our ideas, our thunder, or our power and then feign empathy for our circumstances. So many of you do that. Cut it out.

2) We also know that men and women behave and interact differently. Research proves it, but our day-to-day interactions affirm it. And although women may communicate differently than you do, the core message being communicated is, more often than not, insightful and productive.

I have watched women and men interact for years and have identified several ways that they differ. Women tend to apologize for or qualify everything, while men rarely do either.

Women add qualifiers when they begin to speak in a meeting. Things like, "I have a question," or "Maybe it is just me." While men, on the other hand, come right out and make their statements, self-assured and without qualifiers. Men are very direct, while women are aware that what they have to say could be controversial or not positively received, so they couch their statements in qualifiers.

Women certainly need to become more mindful of *how* they say what they say and try to be more direct. Men need to learn to really listen to the point being made, even if that point is prefaced by a polite or tentative, "Could I say something?" Do not interrupt her, she is probably making a useful point you will want to wait for.

3) Men and women have more in common than some men realize, especially in the workplace. If you listen in on the topics of conversation men have with other men and with women at work, you will hear a marked difference. Because men assume we are more different than we actually are, the conversation starters differ dramatically.

Here is what I am talking about: During casual conversations through the years, my male colleagues tend to ask me about family, travel, or my home. I assume they think that is what I am most comfortable discussing. Yet they will turn to ask my male colleagues to comment on inflation or the yield curve. I do not believe anyone is intentionally trying to insult me, though I do think gendered assumptions tend to characterize the nature of conversation.

And most of those assumptions are invariably wrong.

So, men, you really need to become more self-aware and understand that you are behaving in this way.

Ask a woman the same kinds of business-specific questions you would ask your male colleagues. Push for their opinions on important internal issues at your company. Encourage them to speak up. Ask what they would do differently. Stop limiting conversation to topics you might perceive as more feminine or lightweight and give us a chance to weigh in on more substantive and important topics. We do have informed opinions, some of which you might find useful. Remember, we got the job in the first instance because of the quality of our education and our understanding of the job we are being asked to perform.

4) We are very aware of how painfully slow male-dominated businesses are to accept change. Yes, even with decades of verifiable research suggesting that change would be very beneficial to the enterprise, men really do not want to change. After all, it is so much easier to keep things as they always have been, and actively maintaining the status quo helps retain men's superior position in the corporate hierarchy.

Of late, there is a lot of pressure coming from consumers, regulators, and investors to add more women to corporate boards. Increased scrutiny about board makeup has been evolving for years; however, the COVID-driven social upheaval of 2020 certainly intensified the scrutiny that boards came under. As a result, some modest progress has been made (see the Russell 3000 in CA).

Note I said *some* progress, at least compared to the exclusively male, all-white boards that once ruled virtually all corporate boardrooms. But women and ethnic minorities are still shamefully underrepresented on those boards. Although most intelligent, financially literate people would conclude that corporate board diversity is key to influencing a company's culture, strategic direction and, ultimately, its brand, to say nothing of the understanding of its market, I remain completely baffled. Heavily male-dominated boards and leadership teams continue, unabashedly, to maintain that there has to be some flaw in the research that correlates greater gender diversity with better performance, better credit ratings, and increased consumer satisfaction. You behave, in the face of these irrefutable research findings, as though the conclusions reached and published were part of some passing social movement or fad. Worse, you appear to harbor some conception of the research as one part of a conspiratorial plot to undermine the stability and seaworthiness of the good ship *Corporate*. You say, "We need proof." You say, "Why fix something that is not broken?" Further, you say, "Even if we wanted to bring on more women, where would we find them?"—as if finding them is difficult.

How about you acknowledge the integrity of this research? How about you look a little harder to find those female candidates we both know are out there in droves? Maybe consider altering your talent pipeline and watch as women leaders emerge—because they will. Also, stop using your classic excuses to preserve the board status quo: bad timing and slow turnover. I have been approaching companies for years to inquire about board positions. The favored response? *"You'd be terrific, but, unfortunately, there are no openings on our board."* Address the actual issue, find a way to get competent women on your board now, and reap the benefits of the different perspectives and inputs they will bring. Parroting the old golf adage, "slow your swing down and enjoy the extra distance," let women help you realize the myriad of benefits that will unfold with their engagement. But how, you ask, could you initiate a solution to this ongoing issue? How about simply creating space on the board if there are currently no board openings? Not unheard of. And isn't that what companies do when they identify a high performer they want in their employ? They hire them and then create a new role. How about creating or redrafting board term limits? How about internally mandating and adopting the concept of board gender parity? If you do not get with the program, your companies may be missing material opportunities for growth and stability. It is time to do something now. Plan into it.

So, while we anticipate slow progress, do yourself, your employees, your shareholders, and your bank account a favor. Giddy up, for God's sake.

Are We Making Progress?

And speaking of progress, the Nasdaq stock exchange recently adopted a rule requiring listed companies to add at least two diverse directors to their board or explain why they cannot (which, of course, sounds ridiculous as a statement when you simply say it out loud). And after many years of discussion, California passed a law requiring publicly traded California companies to add two or three diverse directors by the end of 2021.

It was a great start in California. And then, shockingly, in 2022, the law was struck down. A so-called nonpartisan group challenged the idea of a mandated diversity policy for corporate boards as discriminatory?! Apparently, it could possibly discriminate against the old white guys who are now an identified race in California. In California. Who knew? I wonder which gender kicked up that dust. The argument may have been based on a constitutional law principle, which I understand and accept, but the effect was once again to protect and enshrine the status quo.

I am frequently irritated by published articles, generally published by specific interest groups, suggesting that the benefits of a diverse leadership team are inconclusive and that there is no real evidence. To the contrary, if one bothered to look at the readily available peer-reviewed published research or, simpler yet, conduct a simple Google search, they will find the research results there. It is overwhelmingly supportive of gender-diverse boards and corporate leadership teams, which may be why men want to pretend it doesn't exist. The data is hiding in plain sight—there to be found if you were even mildly interested. So, you can certainly ignore those findings, you can choose not to do the research, but that will not change the fact that study after study has documented the positive impact women have in the workplace at every management level, including at the board level.

Just because you do not like the conclusions reached, it does not make the results any less true. So, think of this as new information to factor into making better and smarter decisions. Always remember, the only bad news is the news you didn't get. Now you know, you've heard the news, so no reason not to react to the news you got.

In the face of this hard data, you need to accept that it is entirely probable that you have not done enough to bring women into leadership positions. The good news (now that you have the data and access to the research) is that you can start immediately to make practical, real change in your company. Right now. No time like the present.

Do not misunderstand me or my intent. I believe corporations want the best management team and board that can deliver the best results for stakeholders or shareholders, and they want to enhance the value of the organization. I also believe that diversity is not something you seek because you want more positive public relations or because it is the nice or the politically correct thing to do in the moment. You must diversify your board or your executive team because you want to fill out the mix of skills, perspectives, and experiences the company needs to succeed in its business. But I would say that there are few industries today that are not being impacted daily by the cultural shift, an increasingly diverse population, and an evolving gender fluidity in our new demographic. You need to ask yourself: Why is your company or organization not doing anything to evolve into this new reality? And if you are, are you doing it deliberately, mindfully, and aggressively? Lastly, will you remain committed?

If you are not open to change, you then become the problem! Tell yourself, if you must, that you are acting out in latent, but in this case, late arriving self-interest.

JUST THE FACTS, SIR.

- Gender diversity is associated with increased sales revenue, more customers, and thus potential for higher profitability, reported the *American Sociological Review.*

- Adding just one more woman in a firm's senior management or corporate board is associated with eight to thirteen basis points higher return on assets, the International Monetary Fund discovered.

- Gender-balanced teams were the most likely to experiment, be creative, share knowledge, and fulfill tasks, NCWIT research reported. The study also found that the most confident teams had a slight majority of women (60 percent).

- Team performance peaks when the percentage of women in a business team is 55 percent, UC Berkeley's research found.

CHAPTER 5

You Think You're Not,
But You Are

YOU FINALLY GET THE CHANCE FOR SOME DOWNTIME AND DECIDE to spend the day at the lake on your boat. You make a list, you load the car, pack food and drinks, pack swimsuits and towels, get the lifejackets situated, and off you go. It's a great, relaxing day, right? It is until you realize you forgot the ice and SPF 50 sunscreen. Damn. You thought you were so organized. But now you are stuck with warm beer and third-degree burns on your back. You thought you had done everything possible to ensure an amazing time on the water, but it only took a couple of missteps to ruin the day.

It's the same thing with supporting women. You can do the research, devise a plan, organize programs, and execute on your decision to support women differently in your company. But it only takes a couple of missteps for your best intentions to be ruined.

Not to sound ungrateful, but research shows us that men think they are more supportive in these situations than they actually are. Nonprofit Promundo reports that while 77 percent of men claimed they were doing "everything they can" to support gender equality at work, conversely, and very telling, only 41 percent of women agreed that the men's self-perception was, in fact, the case. What those numbers say to me is that you may *think* you are helping women out, but you are not *really* helping us out in any material way—meaning by that, in a way that is actually contributing to the recognition of our real worth to the organization and to the advancement of our careers.

Instead of giving us lateral movement, which is movement that doesn't elevate us in the hierarchy unless it is part of a plan to prepare us for elevation within the company, you are just moving things around like a little kid trying to hide his spinach under his mashed potatoes on his dinner plate. My intention here is to try and help you really think about how you define doing "everything [I] can." Some of this may be hard to hear, but we'll all be better for it. Stay with me here a little longer. Trust me.

It is true that there may be a small group of you out there making a serious effort to bring about positive change for women. Unfortunately, there are still millions more of you out there who haven't moved off the proverbial dime.

Researchers Colleen Ammerman and Boris Groysberg, in their work on this subject, found that there are far more of you who are apathetic or, worse, indifferent about gender equality. Their writing on this issue concludes that men "without necessarily meaning to, stymie women's advancement." In fact, this is what is happening. Their book, *Glass Half-Broken: Shattering the Barriers That Still Hold Women Back at Work*, addresses the importance of having men like you speaking out and effectively declaring themselves as allies for change to occur, or at least for some progress to be made. Put in the context of all the change that is currently afoot, it is not a big "ask," but it sure seems like so many of you think it is.

We know from an abundance of research that the majority of men in corporate organizations are really not concerned about gender equality issues. This makes sense since you are NOT the ones who are disadvantaged. The "Engaging Men: Barriers and Norms Report," a research paper from Catalyst in 2022, reported that 74 percent of interviewees said that many men are unconcerned, with some suggesting "that men are less aware of the issues around gender bias because they have never been part of an oppressed group." It stands to reason that if you are unaware of gender bias or have trouble understanding it because you have never personally experienced it, you may be skeptical that change is needed. Only 8 percent of men, versus 24 percent of women, believe their gender has made them miss out on a raise, promotion, or chance to get ahead. This is data from Sheryl Sandberg's book *Lean In* and research by the highly regarded McKinsey & Company. And maybe that is why progress appears to be stalling—because you think there has been enough progress. But let's back up a bit.

Because you haven't been the underdog, I understand why you might not fully get what it feels like to be on the receiving end of bias. Here is a little mental game you can play to check your bias: Picture, if you will, being invited to attend a women's conference where you are the *only man* attending. As a result, you have to make small talk with the female executive attendees for two or three hours by yourself. Picture these women asking you only about your family, or where you like to vacation, or how you like the food they're serving at this conference. Meanwhile, all around you in other discussions you are not a part of, women in groups are discussing the stock market, the latest financial legislation, corporate investments, the new golf swing suggested by their teaching pro.

And just when you think it can't get worse, you hear, "Oh, listen, Honey, if you're going to get yourself a refill at the bar, can you grab me another Scotch and soda? Thanks, Sweetie. You're a doll." Breaking through the mind-numbing, never-ending chit-chat would be frustration and anger that sits in the pit of your stomach like a Tums made of battery acid. I speak from experience. Well, remember that little mental game the next time you see the few women attending a male-dominated conference or meeting. Yeah, "Oh!" That's how they feel.

As recently as 2016, most men actually thought that women no longer faced significant obstacles in the workplace, according to Pew research. Yes, despite the fact that women state that discrimination makes their lives harder, you refuse to believe it. When one of your male coworkers tells you he wants a shot at that promotion that just opened up after Ralph announced his retirement, the likelihood is that unless you wanted the job, you would probably say, "How can I help?" or "I'll put in a good word for you," right? Would you do the same for a woman coworker if she expressed interest? Would it even occur to you to do so? I am thinking probably not. Women run into this kind of deeply ingrained bias constantly. To you, it seems like a little thing. To us, it is career sabotage with a very serious and long-lasting impact on our future work and life experience.

You have to wonder if companies are starting to give up on equity for women. I know I am certainly questioning how important it is to most corporations, especially after a recent report from IBM found that even after being made aware of the challenges working women face, "gender equity is still not a top priority for 70 percent of global businesses." This is true even in organizations where leaders claim gender inclusivity is a top business priority. You only need to look at the results to confirm the findings are accurate. Knowing that we increase profits and make businesses stronger, you still do not seem to care. What is with that?

Interestingly, that same study also underscored how women provide an advantage to companies that "view gender inclusivity as a driver of financial performance." Yet another affirmation of what I am trying to communicate in this book. However, almost inexplicably, while saying in one breath that gender inclusivity is a driver of performance, of those companies surveyed, only 11 percent had declared the advancement of women a formal business priority. Yes, you read it correctly, 11 percent. Perhaps now you understand why women continue to feel defeated and frustrated by your inability to act on the overwhelming and conclusive data that says women make a very real and positive difference in the corporate environment. More importantly, however, the presence of women in leadership within that group, called "First Movers," gave those organizations a sizeable advantage. The male CEOs of First Movers self-reported as much as a 61 percent higher mean rate of revenue growth than the 89 percent of companies that had not made women in leadership a stated priority. Clearly, again, women in leadership means more money for the business organization.

Yet it is simply not happening, or most certainly not at the rate that all of the empirical data indicates that it should be. You need to wonder as an owner, as an investor, as an incentivized employee—what is being left on the table unharvested, unrealized, unearned, and undistributed?

And when you hear stories like Mary Ellen's, it can seem like men are not thinking about elevating women *at all*. Mary Ellen had a master's degree in healthcare management and two years with her employer in multiple positions before assuming the role of recruiter, which she did because it had bonus potential over and above her salary. She was a strong performer. More than a year later, Ted and Randy were hired into the recruiter role alongside Mary Ellen due to the company's continued expansion. All three were known as rising stars.

Yet when Henry, the group manager, announced his retirement, only Ted and Randy were asked to apply for the promotion by the senior vice president. This was despite the fact that Ted had been with the company just three months and Randy only four. Apparently, seniority was not a factor for this company, but gender clearly was. Through some digging, Mary Ellen learned that the senior vice president's track record of only promoting men clarified her situation. He had, in fact, *never* promoted a woman.

She is now looking for new opportunities elsewhere where she has a chance at being promoted. I hope that as you are reading this, you keep asking yourself questions like, "What would I feel if the roles were reversed?" "How would I respond if that happened to me?" I think it's critically important that you begin the practice of empathizing with our stories. It's only then that you will really begin to understand why we are asking for fairness in matters of gender equality.

Systemic Roadblocks

Women are being stopped from advancing in ways large and small. The big ways are often systemic roadblocks or obstacles that have evolved, perhaps even were designed, to prevent women from having the opportunity to ascend to the same types of leadership roles men hold. These blocks have been built into the corporate ecosystem, into the larger society, and can only be overcome with your help and support. After all, it was men like you, or your predecessors, who designed the existing model, so it is men like you who can reshape it.

The "Engaging Men" Report cited Sacha Thompson, founder of Equity Equation, who addresses the different diversity strategies members of the tech industry have tried to implement to promote women, but she says that those strategies are bound to fail. "Many of the diversity strategies for tech roles create opportunities for women to excel but do not complete the process by restructuring the environments to be inclusive for women," she says. Without those systemic structural changes, women will continue to be left behind or excluded in spite of the considered strategies and determined efforts of capable women. Men remain the gatekeepers at the end of the day.

Thompson identified three ways that organizations allow systemic roadblocks to continue to exist:

1. Strategy focused more on mentorship than sponsorship
2. No sanctions or penalties for continued gate-keeping behavior
3. Succession planning not tied to accepting and encouraging diversity efforts

Just so we are clear: Being a mentor, sharing knowledge about a client, or explaining how things are done at your company every once in a while, or even every day, is a great start, but *it is not enough*. You need to become a sponsor to the women in your company. You need to become an advocate for her, put her name out there for promotions, talk her up when she is not in the room, give her credit for work she *has* accomplished to other senior leaders you work with.

Mentoring takes her to the fifty-yard-line. Sponsoring gives her the shot at the touchdown, and that is all we are asking for. Do not do this by halves. It is critical for our advancement.

We witness women being repeatedly overlooked for promotions they have earned and deserve, as job openings are systematically filled with less experienced, less qualified men. It happens every day. And it continues to happen every day because there are no consequences for a guy giving another guy a promotion, even when he is not the best candidate. The woman working one office down is and, far too often, you know that. And this is why we're seeing no meaningful progress at all in getting women up and into senior leadership roles.

Why succession planning is not tied to diversity efforts is incomprehensible to me. It is the simplest thing to do. If a board member or the man in the C-suite is retiring or getting fired, replace them with a woman until there is parity. Boom! Done and done. The key here is follow-through. Finish the job.

But back to Sacha Thompson and Equity Equation:

She argues that until companies adjust their diversity efforts "to provide opportunities and ensure women are not tokenized as 'diversity hires' but seen as valuable assets at the table (inclusion)," there will be little shift in workforce demographics.

Exactly.

Tokenization and a Total Lack of Awareness

Being the token woman in the room is like being a unicorn in a barn full of horses. It is not easy. It can be uncomfortable being the lone member of your gender. Now imagine what it feels like to be the only woman in a senior management position. The challenges are many and the opportunities few. It also creates a lot of pressure to be the sole member of the other gender in a management team.

You have no idea what it is like to walk into a meeting a few minutes early or into a corporate cocktail event consisting of 98 percent men, who are all talking sports or the gender equivalent of man talk. From a woman's perspective, the experience is like watching two dogs sniffing each other in an effort to determine who among them is the Alpha Dog. I honestly cannot recall a time when I joined a group and the conversation shifted to a more inclusive topic, which could be anything from local news, to current events, or even the stock market. Continuing to talk about subjects that few women would be interested in is exclusionary and, yes, rude.

Being the token woman in senior management means I'm pretty much invisible until I make my presence clearly known. I personally haven't had a problem with this for a very long time, but do you have any idea what it was like for me in the early days, listening to a group of clueless men talk about how they played a round of golf on Saturday morning and then napped for three hours in the afternoon—while they have two kids under the age of five at home being cared for by their wife who also works Monday to Friday?! And I'm standing RIGHT THERE! Beyond oblivious and, tellingly, a measure of the emotional intelligence of the average male under age sixty-five.

My friend Amanda, a single working mom, vented to me about this very thing. You want to know what most corporate token working mothers' weekends are like? I'll tell you. According to Amanda, this is a typical weekend for her:

She gets awakened at the crack of 5:00 a.m. by her youngest, who wet his bed. She changes his sheets and pajamas and tries to go back to sleep. Can't. Decides sleep isn't an option, makes coffee, has taken all of two sips when her oldest walks into the kitchen demanding to be fed (because she "wasn't tired" and didn't see the need to go back to bed, but "was starving"). Amanda serves her cereal only to be told "it sucked," so she makes scrambled eggs, "but not runny." Okay, dry eggs coming up.

Coffee's now ice cold, so she throws it into the microwave and sits down again to drink it. At that very moment, her youngest comes down requesting eggs: "the kind that look like a yellow eye." Okay, got it! Yellow eye, it is. Coffee cold. Again. Microwave. Again. Gets asked a kagillion questions that she can't answer about caterpillars. Tells them to get dressed for soccer practice while she tries to shower and answer a million more questions through the closed bathroom door about underwear location and jerseys that are still dirty and "gross." (Damn! okay, that one's on her.)

While driving to soccer practice, she hears a "ding" on her phone, but she can't text and drive with the kids in the car, so she waits until they leave skid marks out of the back seat to join their friends on the pitch. As she checks her email, she sees the message is from her boss about a work project that Amanda had asked about the day before during work hours*(!). However, Amanda doesn't have the documents on her phone, so she can't answer her boss until she gets home and fires up her computer.*

After watching her sweet angels run around kicking a black-and-white ball for two hours, she schleps them over to their friend's house for a play date while playing Henry Kissinger to the Middle East Conflict raging in the back seat because of who-knows-what. She then runs home, responds to the boss's email (WHICH WE ALL KNOW SHOULD HAVE BEEN HANDLED YESTERDAY), *runs to the grocery store because those last two eggs this morning were basically all that was left in the way of food, unless you count the rubber celery and half a bottle of salad dressing in the refrigerator door. She feels responsible for this and bad about it.*

On the way home, she realizes she's been driving on fumes, so she stops and gets gas. Gets home. Puts away the groceries. Throws a load of laundry into the washing machine (wet sheets). Pretends to vacuum for a bit but, really, she's just picking up the bigger chunks because who has time?! Leaves to go pick up the kids, and this time she remembers BOTH of them, not like the last time. Don't ask. Makes kids change out of their dirty jerseys and starts another load of laundry. Checks to see if the boss has received her email. Gets dinner started: "Yes, frozen pizza, again." Changes loads of laundry. Tries to fold a fitted sheet. Gives up. Rolls it into a ball and shoves it in the bottom of the linen closet. Cleans up after dinner. Spots some big pizza crust crumbs. Kicks them further under the table because she's not dragging out the vacuum, again. Puts on Frozen. *Again. Millionth time. She hates Elsa with a passion of a thousand burning suns by this point, but it keeps the kids on "stun" in front of the TV and not fighting. Checks emails, again. Still no response. Opens a bottle of red and starts to read.*

Frozen's over, fighting begins. Pop-in Frozen II. *"Stun," again. By third glass of red, it's bedtime for kids. The thirty-minute battle begins. "Yes, you have to brush your teeth so they don't fall out of your mouth." "Yes, it's true that you won't grow taller if you don't get to sleep in the next ten minutes," she swears. Gets them tucked in. Pours the dregs of the bottle into her glass. Checks email, again. Still no response. Goes to bed. AND THIS WAS JUST SATURDAY. Then on Monday, her boss (who never responded to her email) has the balls to be talking about how much fun and rest he got over the weekend??!!*

Put yourself in your wife's or partner's shoes for a second and think about what an ass you sound like before you continue telling us how relaxing and fun your weekend was. The women around you may be rolling their eyes or shooting daggers as they recall their own, which was not nearly as relaxing or fun as yours, let me assure you.

Good job for allowing a woman to join your team, but if she is the only one, or part of a small minority, there is still more work to be done. One or two women does not equal system change; they are still just tokens—a meaningless gesture or weak attempt to signal that your company is doing its part to support the advancement of women. Women can see through the facade. Until women make up 50 percent of the ranks of managers, directors, vice presidents, and the C-suite, you have not done enough. When that happens, a very large part of Amanda's story could be rewritten, though not all of it, because Amanda is still a very conscientious employee and she will always be a mother to those two kids. So even small steps taken to remedy the inappropriate gender work/life imbalance can deliver meaningful change to someone in Amanda's position.

Some men think any progress, even minute, is sufficient. I say that because almost half of men think women are well-represented in leadership when one in ten senior leaders in the company is a woman. The book *Lean In* and McKinsey's "Women in the Workplace" found that fully 50 percent of men think that when corporate leadership is 10 percent women, that is good enough. By comparison, 28 percent of women thought that was sufficient. That even 28 percent of corporate women find that sufficient gender balance is terribly disappointing to me, but again, I know that because expectations have been crushed for so long, even after so much effort and attention has been given to the issue, it may be understandable, if not acceptable, that some women grasp on to that statistic as some form of progress. When is 10 percent of anything considered meaningfully "representative"?! Seriously, do you want to take home only 10 percent of your paycheck? How about 10 percent of a candy bar? Only being allowed to watch 10 percent of the Super Bowl? Yes, 10 percent sucks. Do better. Now.

While widescale change is needed, it is hard to bring that about when men are constantly positioning to hold women back in the workplace with their offhand snide and sexist remarks. Those glib and backhanded compliments are microaggressions, and they may be an even bigger challenge than the systemic roadblocks.

Microaggressions

I am sure you have heard the term "microaggression," but you may not recognize when you are actually behaving aggressively. Columbia Professor Derald Wing Sue defines microaggressions as:

> "The everyday slights, indignities, put-downs and insults that members of marginalized groups experience in their day-to-day interactions with individuals who are often unaware that they have engaged in an offensive or demeaning way."

Sixty-four percent of women report that microaggressions are a daily reality at work, according to LeanIn.org and McKinsey. And I suspect that the other 36 percent who didn't report being on the receiving end probably were but just didn't consciously register it. The transgressions are subtle, and maybe even unintentional sometimes, but the result is that women get knocked down, insulted, and belittled to the point that their efforts to self-promote and to be promoted are sabotaged. Every. Single. Day. Not sure if you have been displaying microaggressions? Here are some of the most common forms:

Interrupting a Woman When She Is Speaking

Is it overconfidence or sexism? Men are generally very comfortable jumping into conversations, especially when women are a part of the group. You don't seem to hesitate to talk over us even when you have no particular expertise at all to share. In fact, it is so common that the phenomenon has been named "manterruptions." Research conducted by Perceptyx in 2022 found that one out of every five women (19 percent) report that they regularly are interrupted or talked over by men in meetings frequently, and more than twice that number (42 percent) say it happens "at least sometimes." The result is that women become less engaged in their work. Wouldn't you be if you were constantly interrupted while trying to make a point or offer a suggestion in a business setting?

Unfortunately, even women in leadership positions are more likely to be interrupted or spoken over, LeanIn.org and McKinsey reported. Thirty-six percent of senior female leaders, versus 15 percent of male senior leaders, report being manterrupted while speaking to a point in a business meeting.

Now, part of this seems to be a product of our socialization. Men interrupt other people (both men and women) twice as frequently as women; however, you are also three times more likely to interrupt women than you are to interrupt men. And that is where the problem lies. Because it is a signal that "Women's expertise simply isn't valued as much as that of men," CNN reported. The quintessential example of this, watched by tens of millions of people, would be Kanye West snatching the microphone out of Taylor Swift's hands at the 2009 MTV Music Video Awards. Cringey, right? (Of course, the antithesis is Congresswoman Maxine Waters "reclaiming her time" when former Treasury Secretary Steve Mnuchin refused to answer her question directly. Mnuchin tried to waste Waters' time with platitudes, and she was not having it, stopping him from talking as she took back the right to ask questions by "reclaiming her time.")

Fortunately, there is a simple solution: Let us speak. Listen to what we are saying and wait until it is clear that we have finished making our point before you start talking. Equally importantly, if you see someone else man-terrupting, be an ally and tell them to wait and let us finish. In these business settings, men are not the only ones with something relevant, important, perhaps critically important to say. Do you ever wonder what gets missed, what gets left unheard, that may have been exactly what needed to be heard, understood, and acted upon? It's not just the woman who suffers when she is interrupted or ignored. The company also suffers by not hearing all of the information she wanted to share. I'm going to add here that women also need to get to the point faster. You don't need a long and involved wind-up to state your thoughts. Get to the point. You'll keep everyone more engaged in the thoughts you're presenting. (That goes for you too, guys.)

Manterrupting is not to be confused with mansplaining, which is when a man feels the need to restate what a woman has just said, as if she did not communicate it clearly enough. Bropropriations occur when a woman shares an idea, it is overlooked, and later a man takes ownership of the idea, restating it as his own, and it receives a positive response that he claims credit for. Another big problem.

All of these behaviors are staggeringly irritating, and they make a woman want to take off one of her stilettos and puncture your left eye. These habits make you look like an ass in a room full of people sensitized to this nonsense. It raises the question, Are you feeling the need to demonstrate your manhood? Your worth in the room? Rationalize your job title? Put whatever pair of pants you want on these behaviors, and no matter what, they do not look good on you. Think big pimple on your fourteen-year-old chin. Everyone is looking at you but not hearing you. Just seeing the big pimple. Ouch.

Speaking of Mansplaining

How you communicate with me or about me tells me how much or little you value me as a woman and as a business professional. If you comment on or explain something to me in a condescending, overconfident, and often inaccurate or oversimplified manner, you are mansplaining. I know you may find it hard to believe, but as often as not, I *do* know more than you do, or I may have a point of view about something you would do well to consider.

I know many women—professionals and experts—who are routinely seen or treated as less credible than the so-called alpha men in business settings. Sadly, the result is that women become reticent to speak up or if they do speak up, sense they are not being heard. This, in turn, drives women into silence, just as it does many men in similar circumstances.

Two things happen: 1) Mansplaining leads women into self-doubt and artificial self-limitation, and 2) mansplaining re-enforces men's longstanding, unsupported, overconfident, and overreaching behavior. These are very often subtle things—could be an ill-timed interruption or maybe an unasked for and unnecessary explanation that makes us wonder if we are being patronized. No matter what, it certainly conveys a skewed message and creates an unwanted impression of us to the room at large.

I will never forget when a male colleague—a young guy and a new father—went on and on during the small talk during a management lunch about how he considered himself some kind of expert on breastfeeding because he had watched his wife breastfeed their babies. Meanwhile, there were three young women there with firsthand experience, all of whom had small children and who, of course, sat silent. Two things were clear: 1) He was no expert, and 2) he was a jackass.

Calling a Woman Aggressive, or a "Ball-Buster"

Consider an example I take from the Netflix series *House of Cards*. Frank Underwood is considered strategically ruthless, but his wife, Claire, whose behavior is just as ruthless, is considered a bitch. We can all guess who gets ahead further and faster… and it certainly is not the bitch, though she is likely better qualified.

We are forced to break with our intuitive selves and then adopt the "man code," which is to be competitive, to practice and act out command-and-control, to accept that only winning matters, to never show your underbelly or any vulnerability, and to never, never, ever worry about who you have to step on to get the job done. Competitive sports and gaming analogies predominate—again, where men dwell. Women do not operate out of this "man code," but if they have ambition, they are wise to understand the elements of that code and learn how to navigate in it, through it, and around it. Women are not that interested in adopting this behavior, and they shouldn't. If a woman tries to emulate any of these "leadership success attributes," she is, more often than not, considered difficult or a bitch, neither of which furthers her career. Here's a test for you: Next time you listen to a male speaker at a conference, note how long it takes to hear the first sports analogy. Then listen to a female speaker. Yup, you'll be waiting for hell to freeze over to hear a sports analogy from her.

Corporations were built by men for men, and the corporate cultures we live in today were built with the man code at its core. That simply needs to be undone and changed. Too much money is being left on the table by you guys.

Boys' Nights Out or Weekend "Bonding Trips"

You men are certainly welcome to socialize with whomever you choose. Your personal life is your own and it is not our business. However, we all know that it is common for work and social life to overlap, especially at senior management levels. Excluding women socially makes it harder for us to advance career-wise. Sure, you can claim you do not deliberately leave us out or assume we would say "no" if you invited us, but the only way to be sure is to *ask us*! Men are not doing enough inviting; to be honest, we both know you are terrible at asking. I know because, overwhelmingly, women report feeling left out simply because they weren't even asked to participate.

A hard fact is that while 81 percent of women say they feel some form of exclusion at work, 92 percent of men do not believe they are excluding women at all, report the authors of *Work With Me: The 8 Blind Spots Between Men and Women in Business*. That explains so much of what is simply wrong about corporate culture. Do men willfully turn a blind eye to these behaviors? Are they the consummate rationalizers of hard truths they don't want to believe about themselves? If so, of course you will be dismissive and will never recognize their behavior as counterproductive. A survey of women in tech in 2016 revealed that 66 percent of women felt excluded from key social or networking opportunities because of gender. So, who's at fault here? Who has the power? Who does the inviting or decides who is going and who is not?

Predictably, some men have begun using the #MeToo movement as rationalization and then justification for avoiding women, saying they are hesitant to socialize with female colleagues "for fear that their motives might be called into question," *Harvard Business Review* found. Not to overstate the obvious, but if your intentions are business-related and you are an ally, you have nothing to fear from including women in social situations. But let's be cynical and say that your intentions are business-related, but the business plan is to keep women outside the castle walls, keep them marginalized away from the corporately essential business networks that you guys covet. Yeah—cynical, right.

Being Told They Are "Not a Good Fit"

Many times, the "fit" excuse is used by an executive to justify not hiring or promoting a woman simply because he is not comfortable around her. In many cases, she is maybe more qualified. Other times, she is more outspoken or articulate. Or maybe she is perceived by you as a threat to your advancement. Those might be legitimate reasons in your mind, perhaps, but no, none of those reasons are necessarily in the best interests of the company that employs you. The decision was made to allay your insecurities about working with a capable woman. So, because the woman is not your college buddy, good old Jeff, *she* is "not a good fit," "not quite the right chemistry for the job," and *she* is passed over. The result too often is that a "Jeff" gets the promotion and she does not, despite her Wharton MBA and excellent on-point job experience. So much for merit if it wears a skirt.

Making Women Jump through More Hoops

Women are consistently asked to jump through more hoops than men in order to qualify or be considered for a promotion. This is because many bosses apparently cannot accept the possibility that women can do the job of men, never mind often stunningly better than a male candidate. So, more tests, more references, more discussions with colleagues.

This is not just my opinion. Women must provide more evidence of their competence than men, the LeanIn study documented. Women are also more likely than men to say that they have experienced the following during the normal course of business:

- Having your judgment questioned in your area of expertise
- Needing to provide more evidence of your competence than others do
- Being addressed in a less-than-professional way
- Often having your work contributions ignored
- Having your ideas appropriated

Again, the solution is simple: Evaluate women using the same criteria as men. Assume they are equally capable, or more so rather than less so. Because that is what is going on here. You are skeptical that a woman could be as strong a candidate as a man, which is why you want to see more proof. You doubt they actually are as qualified. You really need to cut that nonsense out. Once again, you need to ask yourself, What is at the root of this male behavior? From my perspective, this tree root makes for bitter fruit. In nature, that is often a good thing as it tends to let the tree grow undisturbed, much like men doing all they can to keep good women at bay.

The Maternal Wall

I've discussed this earlier, but it is so prevalent it does bear repeating. When a woman becomes a mother, there is the implicit male assumption that her role as a mom takes precedence over all else and that she is no longer a career-oriented or ambitious employee. This is simply not true, as I have already said many times. Women are just as ambitious as ever, even after becoming mothers. And why wouldn't they be?!

The Rockefeller Foundation somehow concluded that 75 percent of men and women surveyed perceived women to prioritize family over career advancement, even when this question about choosing one over the other was never explicitly asked or stated. Again, assumptions are made that are not factual. Women need to be asked the question explicitly, and you need to hear their answer clearly without assuming what the answer will be based on antiquated stereotyping. There is no need for speculation about this.

The problem with this assumption (one problem among many) is that it bleeds into performance evaluations. "Almost 20 percent of white women received comments on their performance evaluations to the effect that they did not want to make partner," the researchers said, although that might rarely or never have been the case. "We suspect that many of these women had not *said* so and that managers were just making assumptions about their diminishing commitment to their work after having children," the researchers stated. It's even worse for people of color. Check out the bullet points at the end of this chapter.

Motherhood becomes a penalty to women because men assume that being a mother is the woman's most important life role. Of note, science is now pretty well convinced that there is no such thing as a "maternal instinct." It is deeply socialized behavior that becomes an assumption that women are first and foremost maternal by nature. Wrong.

Is not fatherhood an important commitment as well? How about the very real economic premise prevalent now that *both* partners must remain breadwinners to support a child and a household out of necessity? Let's extend this new domestic reality and then ask the question: What if a man were denied a deserved promotion because he became a father, and fatherhood was seen as a fatal distraction to competent corporate performance? From a typical male perspective today, it would be considered unfair, unconscionable, sexist, and just plain wrong. Of course, it is equally patently unfair, unconscionable, sexist, and just plain wrong when applied to women in the workplace. So, what happened to the old adage, "What's good for the goose is good for the gander?"

Applying a Double Standard to Women Who Are Mothers

Do you ever notice that when women are interviewed by the press, they often receive questions about how women leaders manage to balance their job and motherhood? Male leaders are *never* asked those questions. By asking women how they can do both jobs well, it infers that something must give, that they couldn't possibly serve effectively in more than one capacity.

This particular double standard is exhausting.

When I am in a social setting (meaning outside of my corporate life) with folks I do not know all that well, how I manage my multiple roles is predictably the same small talk initiated by men (my husband is the exception). They first ascertain what the other men do for a living (they do not even ask me, they just assume I do not work, and if I did, it would not be important enough to talk about) and then usually ask them about sports, cars, musical taste, etc. Me? Once they finally learn that I have had a very full career, with a significant senior position, the inevitable question comes up: "How do you do it all? How do you balance motherhood, a home, and a big job?" It is odd and deeply disconcerting that they seem genuinely to have no expectation that they would have a part in raising children, keeping a home, etc. Even accepting this bizarre parenting philosophy, why don't they ask me even the ridiculously gender-neutral questions like what car I drive, or my favorite brand of vodka, or for God's sake, "How about those Dodgers?"

The same goes for golf. I typically golf with a friend but, on occasion, I will go to a course by myself and end up getting placed in a foursome of strangers. Nine times out of ten, it ends up being three guys and me. By the second hole, I begin to ask the guys what they do (or did) for a living. Astonishingly, 99.9 percent of the time, the guys do not correspondingly ask me what I do for a living. Why is that? I *do*, however, hear them ask each other. It's as if I'm not even there when this happens. As I mentioned earlier, you must work at being more mindful of the women around you and, for goodness' sake, at least try to be more inclusive.

Himpathy

Himpathy, if you have not heard the term before, is the way that powerful and privileged men who behave misogynistically often receive sympathy or concern from their male counterparts. They receive more sympathy than do their actual female victims.

For example, a male colleague might say, "Jeez, Bob, tough break you got spanked by HR just for asking Barbara to get us guys coffee for our meeting. Just because she is a VP should not have made that such a big deal. Sorry, man." Or, perhaps worse, "Jeez, Barbara, sorry about the coffee thing. I did not think you would be so touchy about it or I never would have asked."

Never mind that it was inappropriate to ask Barbara to get anyone but herself coffee in the first place. The sympathy for Bob is so misplaced as to be insulting and cruel. You must see that, most of all, it is symptomatic of a very deep-seated disrespect and disregard for the value of women in the corporate workplace.

The Problem with Benevolent Sexism

Sexism in all its forms is bad for women. Period. But there is one type that is harder to recognize because it frames women in positive ways. It is insidious. It is expressed in compliments about our appearance or personal life rather than highlighting our work accomplishments. Benevolent sexism positions women as inherently fragile, innocent, attractive, and in need of care and protection. Because, after all, we are the weaker sex. That is the implication. Despite its name, benevolent sexism is damaging to women.

There is a pernicious trickle-down effect because the more that women are perceived to be fragile or weaker in any forum, the more that assumptive prejudice is reinforced, and then, as sure as night follows day, the more aggressively the bias is rationalized and then expressed. According to *Harvard Business Review*, "research has also found that benevolent sexism makes it less likely that women will get candid feedback and challenging assignments, and more likely that they will get confidence-eroding offers of unsolicited assistance. All of this undercuts women's perceived competence and makes it harder for them to advance." This benevolent sexism may also be expressed as some ersatz form of protective behavior. Don't give her that tough assignment kind of thinking. The reality? Overlooking women for challenging assignments directly affects their promotability, says MIT Sloan.

So, before you go patting your female colleague on the back for her impressive ability to balance her family AND work life while all the while "looking good," think about the message you are sending. Steer clear of comments that call into question her abilities, experience, or ideas, or suggest in any way that she might need backup. I assure you, she does not unless she says she does—another overlooked female strength. Men? Well, they just tend to crash ahead, seldom reaching out for help. They then do the damage assessment later.

Now, I do not think you wake up in the morning and plan how to devalue a woman's work experience during the day. Quite frankly, I do not think you would be reading this book if you were simply a misogynist. But you can stop yourself from "helping" women with unsolicited and misinformed explanations, especially on things we are more expert on than you have been or will ever be. Just stop it. We will let you know when we need your expert guidance.

JUST THE FACTS, SIR.

- According to 2018 Yahoo! coverage of research from Fatherly, "men are still all kinds of sexist."

- A 2008 Harvard study showed that women are subject to negative backlash for expressing anger in professional settings, while men receive positive responses.

- According to Ipsos, US men are more likely than women to believe that women have the same opportunities for advancement as men; 38 percent of women vs. 47 percent of respondents overall.

- A Harvard Business Review study for one specific law firm found, "that only 9.5% of people of color received mentions of leadership in their performance evaluations - more than 70 percentage points lower than white women."

CHAPTER 6

C'mon, Be a Hero,
Not a Villain

TODAY, MORE THAN EVER, WOMEN NEED MALE ALLIES IN THE workplace. We need you. We need men like you who are willing to use their power and their privilege to support and advocate for us. As you have doubtless seen, we have been trying for many years now, yet we are not making much significant headway on our own. We need men who can help ensure we are seen and our voices are heard, men who are committed to helping elevate women into leadership roles.

However, in order for you to actually help us, it is going to require that you commit, that you are consistent in your commitment, and that you follow through. This is not a "one-and-done" endeavor. You really must dedicate yourself to the idea that women should be at the highest levels of senior management. It must be an openly held commitment, a long-term commitment, or it will not work for either of us. It is my hope that you will see that advocating for the women in your company will not only increase earnings but will change corporate culture in a positive way, companywide.

At the same time, it will also elevate your own profile within your company and send positive messaging to other men in your organization that long overdue change is afoot. This is how you do the right thing and become a memorable leader, a change maker, in your company's history.

Stepping into an advocate role will not only enhance your position as a leader, but it will significantly help the company retain the strong women you may already have on your staff. Without advocates, it is easy to feel hopeless and unwanted at work (voice of experience here). Women who feel alone or unsupported at work are much more likely to jump ship to an organization that *will* recognize, appreciate, and reward their contributions with advancement, or they will float their own boat and perhaps become a savvy competitor. Having both professional and personal connections inside an organization marks the difference between short-term and long-term employees. Women with coworker-allies of both genders have increased job satisfaction and greater loyalty to their employer, according to Greater Good Science Center.

Letting us know that you are with us is a big deal. I am not sure many men can grasp the soul-crushing feeling associated with being underrepresented at work, with being outright ignored or marginalized in meetings, not to mention being passed over for promotions, as we frequently are. Think about it—we work hard at our jobs just like you do, we work harder at building consensus, we bring a different perspective, and, most importantly, we bring a more effective problem-solving aptitude to our work. So, just know this—we know our work is good, so forgive us if we're stunned when we hear you say: "We don't think you are ready for the promotion." Frank's frat buddy with less experience than a woman you work with gets the gig, or perhaps even more galling, Bob's golf buddy has always wanted to work in finance, so "Let's give him a try." You pass us over for someone with less experience because he happens to look just like you and expect us to say, "good pick, well done." I don't think so.

I cannot tell you how frustrating and demoralizing that is for women. It is demoralizing to be ignored, particularly when we know for a fact that we are well-qualified or overqualified for an executive position. Imagine yourself in our shoes for just a moment, if you can. The feeling of disappointment is palpable, and we are made to feel it time and again.

And if you do not think that happens, you are sadly mistaken. It happens all the time. That is why we almost invariably end up asking ourselves why we should work for a company that ignores us. Would you stay at a company that promotes friends, family, or employees less qualified than you, leaving you questioning your abilities, your qualifications, your credentials, and, ultimately, your sense of self-worth? Hell, no! You would be leaving skid marks out the door. But this is what women have been dealing with for decades. Look, happy people are productive people. We are already productive, so make us happy and watch what happens. Actively do something to help us. We will not disappoint.

We cannot compel this change without you. Your involvement is critical for success. Boston Consulting Group (BCG) found that "when men do become directly involved in gender diversity, both men and women believe that their company is making much greater progress in achieving gender parity." Globally, BCG reports, "among companies where men are actively involved in gender diversity, 96 percent report progress. Conversely, among companies where men are not involved, only 30 percent show progress." Fellows, it is the difference between an achievable uphill slog and the seemingly almost impossible ascent of a sheer incline.

In short, *actually doing something* about addressing gender diversity actually works. So, we do need you in order to succeed here. If you are willing to help, we will all win through the better results we will be able to achieve together. If you don't believe this to be true or you're still sitting on the fence about all of this, there is one simple way to prove it to be true. Do it. Commit to gender diversity, if not parity, for twelve months. Watch how much better your business starts to become. Watch how much happier and more productive your employees are. Watch as your bottom line begins to increase. Only then will you really *get it*. Try not to think about all the productive time squandered and the money left on the table.

So, what exactly can you men do to be an advocate and ally? I am glad you asked. There are several things, actually.

Ask How You Can Help

Literally, just ask. Turn to the women on your team or in your company and ask them what frustrates them about your organization and what progress would look like to them. What do they need, or what do they feel is lacking? You might hear they need a champion or sponsor, or maybe they want a formal mentorship program, or even a clear path to promotion. Be assured, they will have recommendations and opinions. What they most frequently do *not* have is access to someone with power willing to listen and help introduce change. When, if ever, was the last time you actually reached out to the women in your organization to ask them that simple question? Mind-blowingly elementary, I know. Lend them your ear.

Suggest Training

I understand that you may be feeling a little overwhelmed, maybe even threatened, by this suggestion, so let's take a step back first. How about talking with HR and suggesting a new training program for the women and men in your organization. The training would start at the senior executive level and then work its way down through the hierarchy after those at the top declare to you their buy-in and commit to you their support for it.

The training would be designed to make sure all management staff (women and men) fully understand the problem of gender inequity and then, as a second component, have them design strategies to help fix it—engage them in researching and imagining possible viable solutions. Then task them with the responsibility of developing effective programs based on those possible solutions. Lastly, and most importantly, empower them to begin the process of implementing change. Remember, once they really grasp the challenges that capable women in their company are facing and being held back by, they should be much more able to implement strategies to address and correct practices that are obstacles to a healthier, more productive and profitable enterprise. Getting everyone to take ownership of this training may be challenging or it may be straightforward; either way, when implemented, its impact will be very significant.

Step Back

Granted, many, if not most of you, may not want to take a step sideways, backward, or down. I get it. But if you really want to experience the power of gender parity and a healthier bottom line, you need to make space for talented women. As a leader and change maker, you may need to create new roles for women to hold. In some cases, that means men have to expect that they could be bypassed for a promotion they may feel they deserve. It is complicated, it is hard, and that is why there needs to be real and dedicated commitment to the process. That does not necessarily mean men need to quit their jobs, however, but it could mean they take a lateral move to allow a woman to be promoted. It is extremely unlikely that men will decline invitations for promotion or even consider standing aside and recommending a better qualified woman colleague in his stead. One workaround: You could direct HR to fill the next available promotion slots (that are not in the HR or marketing department) with women.

Quiet Down

In some cases, women's voices are not heard simply because men's voices are figuratively and literally louder and more persistent. It can be exhausting and not overly productive to try to compete with men who simply have to be heard (or like to hear themselves talk). In many cases, women simply get tired of trying to get a word in and eventually give up. That is not good for the company, however, so how about working very hard to change the culture, suggesting to your male employees they curb their tongues every so often and, at the same time, look for ways to encourage the women in the room to speak up? Maybe even directly ask for their thoughts or opinions in a meeting? I know for many of you, these very deliberate but simple actions will cause angst associated with a new way of conducting your business, but if you do these things, you will be surprised by what will be contributed, and you and your organization will be beneficiaries of this new order as well. They may not be ideas you would have come up with, but that doesn't make them any less valuable. Let women speak, listen, and then analyze. The company will soon benefit.

Do Your Research

Before you start representing yourself as a women's advocate, learn more about the sexism they have had to endure so that you truly get an understanding of what we have been facing for a very long time. Not only will this make you better informed, but it will make you more effective as an advocate and champion for the talented women in your organization. When you have some understanding of what we deal with regularly, you will be better able to avoid similar mistakes in the future. You'll also be more effective at discouraging the offensive behaviors practiced by some of your male colleagues and employees. You do not have to hire a research team to discover what it is like to be a woman working in corporate America today. Ask around. Read some of the published white papers on the issue. Spend the same amount of time you would on any other obstacle or issue that is in the way of your company's growth and success.

Speak Out

Communicate to everyone around you that you are an ally of the women in the company and encourage other men in the organization to join you. Then act the part. Move from ally to advocate. Look for practical and readily noticeable ways to shine a spotlight on the smart women in your organization and proactively find or create opportunities for them to grow and advance. Be clear in your intentions. Be vocal. Become a walking sandwich board for the talented women in your company. Think of it as generating good karma. The company will be rewarded.

Speak Up

When you hear verbal microaggressions or witness any form of discrimination, call it out. Point a finger. Make the men in your circle or in your employ aware of what they are doing and let them know in no uncertain terms that the behavior is not okay. Not because women need protecting but because the behavior is wrong. Period. Point that fact out at every opportunity. As I have said before, many men are just not aware of the toxicity they are creating or spreading; they have not thought much about it and may be acting out of ingrained behaviors almost unconsciously. We need your help getting them to stop by bringing them to a new level of awareness and then to mindfulness in their interactions with your female employees.

Celebrate Successful Women

You may have the most amazing women working in your company, but if no one acknowledges them and celebrates them, it becomes harder for them to get the attention they need to progress and advance. Instead, how about shining a bright light on your talented female employees and making that part of your corporate culture? At a minimum, make sure when you turn that spotlight on the talent in your organization, it illuminates both your female and male star performers.

Speaking of spotlighting, I read about a program at JP Morgan Chase that I think should become a model for spotlighting and elevating talented women. JP Morgan Chase's 30-5-1 program encourages employees "to spend 30 minutes each week meeting with a talented woman, 5 minutes congratulating a female colleague on a win, and 1 minute praising that woman to other colleagues." Imagine what a difference it would make if everyone was responsible for identifying, getting to know, and championing women on a regular basis?! And just so the point isn't missed: Clearly, JP Morgan Chase recognized the reality of the issue in the corporation. Someone listened, someone acted. Perhaps change really is afoot at JP Morgan Chase.

Invite Feedback

Even men who are entirely on board with helping women out often realize they do not always get it right, or they may be fearful of misstepping or misstating something. You might have experienced this yourself. So, rather than putting your foot in your mouth, ask the women who are sitting right next to you for the best way to phrase something or how to best communicate your point. You might begin with, "I could use your help in ensuring I am expressing this appropriately." Or "if I say something that sounds biased or sexist, please point it out to me so that I can be more aware and avoid repeating the same mistake." You are much more likely to receive useful guidance and to be seen as the ally you aspire to be. And word will quickly get around. The positive goodwill soon follows you, and that goodwill transfers to your bottom line.

Forge Relationships

More than anything, we need you to *do something*. It is great if you can voice support and encourage other men to follow your lead but then we need you to propose that a woman be promoted, be added to the board, be given a great professional development opportunity, be asked to present to a management committee, attend an industry conference as your representative—the list goes on and on. We need you to become a catalyst for change, which is easier to do when you can speak from personal experience about the amazing women in your company. So, get to know the women on your team, be able to articulate their strengths, and then become their advocates. And be practical. Make a deal with yourself that you are going to help the women you work with get five minutes of facetime with someone higher up in the corporate food chain twice a week, forever. Or, if you are at the top of the hierarchy, make a point of setting aside some time to be available for that facetime with a woman identified as a qualified candidate for a senior executive position. Once again, it is critical to set personal advocacy goals for yourself so others in the organization see that it is important to you and, in turn, for the company you run or manage the financial outcomes for. This really is something practical that you have to do. In short, you must do something more than pay lip service to the idea that women will add value and that gender parity is a goal worth striving and driving for.

My friend Pam had the good fortune to forge a professional connection with a director at her corporation who took note of her advanced degree and her smarts. He took her under his wing, became a champion for her, and persuaded other men in leadership to advocate for her advancement as well. He spoke out, and then he took opportunities to encourage the hiring of more women and promoted the elevation of women into more senior roles.

He was able to do that by paying attention to everyone in meetings and workshops and then striking up conversations with junior employees who had interesting ideas. Those professional conversations turned into lunch meetings and then career strategy sessions. He made it a personal mission to try to bring his Fortune 500 employer into a modern paradigm by upping the percentage of women in leadership roles. In doing so, he became known as a leader who excelled at spotting raw talent.

Push for Better Policies and Use Them

Advocate for workplace policies that make that balancing act most women must undertake easier. Many of these policies have been around forever, such as flex time, remote work, fair pay, pay transparency, and paid family leave, just to name several that directly help level the playing field. These policy shifts may benefit women most because of all the many hats we must wear, but to reduce the impression of an advantage being given to women associated with these policies, more men need to take advantage of them as well, in particular, flex time, paid family leave, and remote work. If this were to happen, it would have a positive effect on the family construct women have historically been accountable for, too. So, fellows, if these policies are in place in your shop, use them for yourself. Work remotely when you need to, or if it would be more expedient and economical for you and the company, insist on pay transparency and take advantage of parental leave for your family's sake so that it is not seen as a policy specifically for women. Help make it clear that everyone needs a more flexible workplace, not just women. Because these policies *do* benefit everyone, including the children in families of working parents.

Share Information

Women are often at a disadvantage because they are not part of the "old boys network." They do not pick up on *the buzz* about salaries, upcoming job openings, and other opportunities the male rumor mill keeps itself fully apprised of. So, share what you know. Be open about your salary and help your female colleagues achieve pay parity. You know you cannot possibly rationalize why your female peer is earning less than you are for doing the same or more work than you do.

Instead of withholding the information, by way of example, let them in on the scuttlebutt that Bill, the head of sales, has taken a job elsewhere and his job will need to be filled. This is a very critical element of the kind of change in attitude and behavior being contemplated here. We need you to let us in on the secrets you guys are whispering about. The whispering emanates from on high and we are not part of that "chat line." Without this kind of insider information, women will be hard-pressed to get into the race for meaningful advancement.

Stop Pretending There Is Not a Problem

Many years ago, when I first spoke at conferences and symposia about the "woman problem" and told everyone present why corporations needed to prioritize getting more women into leadership roles, lots of my fellow CEOs nodded in agreement. Beyond it simply being the right thing to do—good enough reason on its own for many of us—I shared how the different perspectives that women leaders bring to the table improve corporate performance. I also laid out the demographic, societal, and workplace trends that pointed to what we now refer to as DEI needing to become a strategic priority for all enterprises.

Despite the head-nodding and apparent agreement, many in these largely male audiences, when pressed, simply refused to believe we had a problem, citing my presence (and the few other women in the room) as evidence. Some even recoiled at my insistence on gender balance and delivered some variation of "What? Are you suggesting we need some sort of (insert nervous cough or breathless sputter) affirmative action?"

At the time, I truly believed formal affirmative action policies would not be necessary, as more people, acting out of enlightened self-interest, would naturally come to understand that if they addressed the "issue," the corporation would benefit, as would the majority of women who aspired to advance in their careers. And I said so. For years. Now, almost two decades later, and many years after Sheryl Sandberg's groundbreaking book *Lean In* was published, very limited progress has been made. Barely any progress, actually.

In fact, we are taking steps backward. The 2022 ruling in the state of California that boards of directors cannot be required to include women, declaring the law unconstitutional, is a major setback to efforts to diversify corporate leadership.

According to the *50/50 Women on Boards Gender Diversity Directory and Index* for 2020, just 4 percent of the 540 financial services firms in the Russell 3000 have gender-balanced boards, 26 percent have just one woman serving, and fully 6 percent have zero women on their boards. Overall, a mere 19.5 percent of board seats in the financial services sector are held by women. Those numbers may also be plateauing, says Equilar, which reported that "women represented roughly 40 percent of new directors added to Russell 3000 boards in the first and second quarters of 2022, down from 41 percent and 47 percent in the same period last year." Meanwhile, women still comprise slightly more than 50 percent of the US population and generally still manage household finances while being either the principal or equal breadwinners.

Any marketing professional worth their salt knows the powerful gender-driven statistics in the marketplace. Who makes the major decisions in the household on homes, cars, schools/education, clothing, groceries? Women do—80 percent of those decisions. So, gents, if you run an organization that manufactures, sells services ranging from medical care, carpet cleaning, intellectual property or general merchandise, widgets or useless gadgets, simply acknowledge how much more successful your business could be if there were simply more women making decisions at the most senior levels.

Quick shower thought: Do you even know how women think about investments or the stock market? If you do not know how we think about finances, how can you possibly tailor a product for us that we might want? The women in your office know, but if you shut them out, *you* will never know. And that, my friend, will unnecessarily and foolishly limit a financial sector or service sector corporation's future revenue.

The story is even more discouraging when we take race into account. Currently, in the US, 60 percent of women are white and 40 percent of women are of color, a racial mix which, by the way, is projected to flip by 2060 to 56 percent non-white women and 44 percent white women. Who is your marketing guru now? Today, white women hold just 32.8 percent of total management positions in the US and, last year, Asian, Black, and Hispanic women together held just under 10.8 percent of those roles (included in the 32.8 percent), according to Catalyst. If you are not doing the math here (and it is not at all complicated) and what you know you should be doing in the years ahead is not yet readily apparent to you, you can stop reading now. You are one of those cavemen I referred to earlier.

We must do better, much better, at addressing the woeful state of our corporate DEI shortcomings—in relation to both women overall and, in particular, to women in our Black, Asian, South Asian, Indigenous, and non-binary populations. They are a material part of your future. You can either get ahead of it or watch as both it and your company fall behind the horizon.

The good things simply will not happen without the cooperation and leadership of men; men like you, I hope. Men who want for their daughters the same opportunities that exist for their sons. In fact, men who will insist upon that occurring. The dawning reality is that men who have power and position now need to prepare to relinquish some of that status or reimagine it to make a space for women overall and for women of color especially. By reimagining, I am not talking about you walking out the door with a career's worth of work in the proverbial cardboard box while a new order settles in. No, not at all. I want you to reimagine you in a different, more relevant, socio-economic, and cultural paradigm. You are absolutely there. But the landscape and maybe the colors of things in your reimagined world are different. Sound exciting? Sound promising? I hope by this stage if you are still reading, you are beyond mildly curious and your eyebrows have settled back into their usual spot on your lofty forehead.

So, please, seriously consider what kind of leader or executive manager you want to be regarded as.

If you are one of those well-positioned, forward-thinking men of goodwill who actually wants to fix the corporate world's "woman gender problem" and help to achieve gender balance in our lifetime, the most impactful thing you can do in the short term is when you are ready to step down and step aside, please champion and recommend a female candidate for your executive position.

Are you serving as a director on a board with too few women? Be a leader and point it out to your fellow directors. If they do not respond as you would hope they would, begin to lobby for an expanded board to provide for the recruitment of qualified women board members only. Let your fellow directors know that you are resigning to make space for more women. But before you go, seek out a female successor and groom her to win your seat. If that fails, you really don't want to be on this Neolithic board. Move on. You will still be my hero, and you will be a hero to the countless women who hear of your attempt to bring that board into the twenty-first century. Lastly, shame them as you go out the door.

And now that you are coaching the team, the next time a colleague asks you to sit on your umpteenth board or industry committee, do not simply acquiesce or beg off the commitment. Tap your considerable professional network to locate a qualified woman to serve instead. Then champion her candidacy and share your insights to help her succeed.

Be assured, the women are out there are qualified to contribute, prepared to lead, and eager to serve. So, if any of you are having trouble locating women to step up, ask yourself about the barriers that are, perhaps inadvertently, discouraging women applicants. Better yet, ask the women in your circles what needs to be done or changed to get them to step up. Then make the necessary changes to facilitate their participation. Help tear down the walls you may once have guarded.

If even only a handful of highly visible male corporate leaders took this sort of bold and collaborative action, their example could reverberate throughout corporate America and have a huge impact. It would also demonstrate to consumers at large that the business you are part of really does operate according to a different and more contemporary set of socio-economic values than your competitors.

I have personally had the privilege of working with a male industry colleague who understood the importance of having more women in senior ranks. Not just to even the numbers or achieve gender equity but because he truly understood the value of the female perspective that was missing at a board table made up primarily of all men. A female colleague of mine and I were asked to meet with him to discuss "the future." We had no idea what he was referring to and, to our surprise, ascertained that he was eager to assist the two of us in getting elected to a very influential board. He explained his concern regarding the attitude at the board table that simply embraced the "way things had always been done" and that it was time for some big change. He was already on this particular board and about to ascend to its executive committee—meaning where all the real power was. He felt compelled to use his reputation and considerable influence and powers of persuasion to get us to that board table.

He had two years of his term remaining on this board and as part of his legacy, he was committed to making this board more diversified—for all the reasons outlined in this book. He understood the significant value that increased diversity would bring in terms of perspective, market representation, talents, aptitudes, attitudes, and values. He was determined to use his credibility to see us succeed. He knew exactly how to make it happen—from campaigning, to endorsements, to avoiding the various pitfalls, to candidate positioning. He had a complete knowledge of the system and the players, who was likely to support and who wasn't, and how to handle each of them. As women who had never been exposed to the inner workings of how board positions were filled, we were both astonished and grateful.

We both ended up on the board, and we did contribute a different perspective just as he hoped we would. We went on from there to work toward parity on that board and in the organization's senior executive ranks. We succeeded and it is a reimagined organization, in step with its constituents and leading the pack of its organizational peers.

So, what do you think? Are you ready and bold enough to either stand aside or stand down so more women can step up, to use your contacts, knowledge of systems, your small "p"— political prowess—and creativity to lift women and help them find their rightful place in leadership?

It Is Time to Value Women's Leadership

The idea that more women in senior leadership roles equates consistently to more financial success for a company is a truth that you really need to just accept because it is a fact now well-established by research and data. Earth is not flat. Let us move on.

As a male leader, you can either ignore this obvious opportunity or you can harness it to improve the top line performance and the bottom-line results of your organization. And as I mentioned earlier, you can become the hero of your company's story. But you need to act.

You need to put an economic value on women's leadership.

The definition of a stakeholder in a corporation has changed significantly over the past decade. It is not just the traditional capitalist ideal of being responsible to shareholders. Now it includes consideration of the role of consumers, their expectations and protection, societal perceptions of the values in place in corporations, and increased governmental and regulatory oversight now placed on a corporation. There is more to be concerned with and addressed, and women at the leadership level can help successfully resolve these concerns.

Men need to reimagine their roles and responsibilities regarding mentorship and sponsorship. We need you to not just be mentors (give feedback, advice); we need you to be sponsors (use your power and influence at the highest level to advocate for women). If the leadership is not yet gender-balanced—half men, half women—or well on the way toward achieving that, then men in positions of corporate authority and influence need to be taking every step necessary to address this. Now.

There. I said it. Men need to step up, step in, step out, step aside, or step down. Boards need to embrace this reality. Corporate boards—public, private, not-for-profits (P3s)—all need to get more comfortable with transparency and be brave enough to examine the truth about diversity. It will not be pretty, I promise you, but do it anyway. That is really the only way you will sustain the necessary movement forward and succeed in the socio-economic cultural present and future. If you want to be around and thriving, you cannot start soon enough.

Creating an Inclusive Environment

But it is not good enough to just *talk* about transparency, you need to demonstrate it. Publicly traded corporations need to make their EEO-1 (Equal Employment Opportunity) report available to every employee, as well as the public, in order to be seen to be holding themselves accountable for their progress (or lack thereof) toward inclusion. Privately held corporations should, whenever practicable, make the same kinds of disclosure to their employees. However, most public or privately held companies will not have the emotional IQ to recognize the inherent value of doing this. They are too afraid of the "optics." The optics would reveal to their shareholders, employees, and the public how they are failing the women who either do or could, if given the opportunity, make the companies thrive. Be the leader who gets the EEO-1 report into every employee's hands. That's the only way to truly engage and begin the process of committing to getting real change happening now. Hold your own feet to the fire. A hard ask, I know. But it is past time.

There is more we need to discuss about the importance of the EEO-1 report and how that information can and should be used to move a company forward toward meaningful inclusion.

Every corporation needs to create an environment where there is the possibility of a very predictable and real epiphany occurring across the organization—that moment when it becomes apparent you woefully lack diversity and you are compelled because you must see your situation for what it is.

Own the circumstances and do something about them. The first thing to do is to get deeply informed about your situation. Then you can begin to be the architect in the creation of a culture of "conscious inclusion"—building the desire, the insight, and the capacity of people to make decisions that will foster inclusivity. Study, think, lead, and then act with the conscious intent of including everyone. This is one of those things that has been a problem for decades, but it is also a problem that really only takes a relatively short time to reverse if approached resolutely.

Because corporately, women have been excluded from the critical decision-making process in this country until very recently so they still only represent a very small percentage of that small percentage of the uppermost echelons of the decision-making hierarchy.

Think about the vast majority of historical movies that were released in the last few years. Those stories were all told from the men's perspective, as if women had no role at all. I am talking about *Dunkirk* and *1917* and *The King's Speech*, to name a handful off the top of my head. With very few exceptions, such as *Hidden Figures* and *Harriet* and *The Woman King*, women are effectively left out of the storyline, except as someone's wife or girlfriend. What we see in the movies reflects everyday life for women even today. We are starting to see some progress, yes, but certainly not the equity we should be seeing at this place in history.

Corporations essentially created by men for men still remain embarrassingly male-centric. Can you imagine a world where women were involved in making the key decisions on policy, priorities, funding, etc.? My bet is they would "go across the aisle" (political party be damned) to do the right thing a lot more often than we see men do today. Education, healthcare, childcare, and the environment would be top priorities. The tone and agenda would change and so too would the general socio-economic effectiveness of governance if women were simply represented in proportion to the actual population and their overall fiscal impact. It is coming. It will happen. You need to be ready for the inevitable impact of more women in the corporate thin air at the top.

Women make up a slight majority of the US population—51 percent—and we are 47 percent of the US labor force. So much for the stereotypical suburban house-bound domestic engineer. We are now better educated in greater numbers at every level of academic and professional certification. Our education and qualifications span every trade, every professional certification, the humanities, to the sciences, to medicine, engineering, nuclear physics, the military, academia, economics, politics, athletics, and the frontiers of space. But what? We do not belong in the CEO's office? We do not belong on a corporate board? We could not possibly chair that board?

Despite the reality at play in the Western economies, the odds remain materially and shamefully stacked against any woman who aspires to leadership. Here we are, a majority of the population and 47 percent of the labor force, yet we represent a paltry 8.2 percent of Fortune 500 CEOs, 7.3 percent in the Fortune 1000, 6 percent in the S&P, and 5.6 percent across the Russell 3000. These, as fact, represent a crushing indictment of men in positions of authority in the corporate sector. Numbers don't lie. Men have and will continue to do everything in their considerable power to hold women in place unless they are disrupted. No one should be surprised. Only hugely disappointed. Is this the person your mother raised you to be?

As stated earlier, women hold more associate degrees, more bachelor's degrees, and more master's degrees than men. And those percentages are most dramatic among young professionals just entering the leadership pipeline—those in their late twenties. According to the Census Bureau, in 2021, 53.1 percent of all women over age twenty-five in the US had received a bachelor's degree, versus 46.9 percent of men, which continues a multiyear trend of women surpassing men in this category. These numbers should bode well as women, and forward-thinking men, push for more women in leadership and the trend continues to bring a great pool of talent to the corporate world. Yet another reason to pay serious attention, gentlemen. So, the next time you find yourself sitting across the table from a woman at a meeting, know that there is a fairly good chance she is at least as well educated as you, perhaps more educated than you and your boss. It's okay, though; you still wear the pants. For the moment.

And what about the cultural stereotypes surrounding different types of jobs? What is a man's job? What is a woman's job? Say you have an opening for a senior position in human resources (HR). Do you expect to choose a woman or a man for that job? How about marketing? Female or male? Now think about your finance vice president or chief financial officer—male or female? As an exercise, will you honestly acknowledge what your inherent initial thought was?

Why can't a man be just as capable in HR or marketing as a woman? Why do we have difficulty accepting that a woman could be a very effective CEO, CFO, COO, or CTO? What could gender possibly have to do with your thinking about filling these positions? Without wanting to be overly dramatic, it has tragically and consistently been my experience that if there are women in senior corporate leadership, you are much more likely to find them in HR and in marketing. Historically and clearly not coincidentally, those departments are among the least likely paths to the CEO's chair or the rarified air of the boardroom.

Meanwhile, it is predominately men we find in functions involving accounting and finance, which, of course, are the typical hunting grounds for boards and the search firms they engage when seeking CEOs, CFOs, COOs, EVPs, etc. It has created a perpetual self-fulfilling prophecy of the male-centric board and C-suite environment that overwhelmingly predominates in our corporate and business environment today. When women are missing from roles in accounting, finance, and other male-dominated departments, it is no wonder they are less likely to be considered for the top dog role or for board seats.

Simple example: Most all of the pilots the commercial aviation industry hired were former military pilots. Women weren't allowed to fly planes in the military until 1976 (or enter fighter pilot training until 1993). Guess who never got a shot at piloting commercial airplanes until the mid-1970s? Yup. Women. The first exception to that was Emily Howell Warner, who was hired by Frontier Airlines in 1973. There is a very direct and consequential correlation between women streaming in the right or the wrong corporate pipeline and getting the top job because that's where the search happens.

Without one, you don't get the other. If you are not within sight, you cannot possibly be seen.

JUST THE FACTS, SIR.

- Harassment and microaggressions are increasing, yet often go unreported. The majority of working women (59 percent) have experienced harassment and/or microaggressions in the last year, which is up from 52 percent in 2021, reports Deloitte.

- That same 2022 Deloitte report found that women working for "gender equality leaders" were far more likely to stay where they were than those working for lagging organizations.

- Having a male ally in the workplace boosts a woman's sense of belonging, according to an article in *Social Psychological and Personality Science*.

- More than ninety countries now have parental leave laws, "Yet, the proportion of men who take more than a few days off work when their child is born is tiny," the BBC reports.

CHAPTER 7

Ya Gotta Start Sometime, so Right Now Would be Good

W E HAVE IDENTIFIED AND DEFINED THE PROBLEM OF WOMEN being underrepresented in the C-suites and boardrooms. We have proposed several solutions to this problem. Now, let's take a look at what companies are actually doing about it and how effective their efforts have been while asking, "Is it enough?" It is no coincidence that this chapter is the shortest in the book. Ouch, right?

Despite the fact that efforts to address the need to increase the number of women in the boardroom are not making much headway *at all* (as I have said earlier), now some companies are at least beginning to take some action. Believing that the first step to getting women into board roles is to get them into senior management, a growing number of corporations are instituting policies to try to energize progress, at least internally. The goal with many of these new initiatives is to attract more educated and qualified women to the organization and then get them on the career ladder and then up into senior leadership roles.

These programs and initiatives are considered "best practices" because they are evidence of tactics that have helped achieve at least some progress. But given that we are nowhere near gender parity on any front, and this now a decade or more after introducing the programs, I think we can all agree that they are more like "good practices," given that material progress has proven so elusive. If they were truly "best practices," we should expect to have made more headway.

However, there are some good ideas that are the basis of these recent initiatives, which may serve at least as a starting point for your organization's efforts.

Companies Leading the Way

Companies like Unilever began making a concerted effort to achieve gender parity back in 2010. In the decade between 2010 and 2020, Unilever went from 38 percent of managers being women to 50 percent globally, with that percentage reaching 52 percent in 2021. The company's work on achieving gender parity is absolutely moving in the right direction and its corporate performance reflects that. In 2022, Unilever reported on its full-year 2021 results: "The acceleration of Unilever's operating performance continues. We delivered our fastest underlying sales growth for nine years—4.5 percent for the full year, with 1.6 percent from volume." This is why you should be doing this. Soon.

The company claimed that its keys to success included leadership from the top, addressing unconscious bias, creating an inclusive culture, facing down hot spots (meaning areas where there is industry-wide underrepresentation of women in management), and fighting existing stereotypes of businesses and brands. Shining a spotlight on inadequate representation seems like it was a strong first step here. I remain curious to see what Unilever does to continue reinforcing and building on its success thus far.

Sodexo took a different tack, tying its senior executive's financial compensation to an increased female presence and, to no one's surprise, it worked well. We all know when money is on the table, desired results can quickly be achieved.

The company's improvements in gender diversity have moved in parallel with improved business metrics, beginning in the early 2000s. Between 2003 and 2010, the number of women in leadership at Sodexo increased by 74 percent, while the number of women on the executive committee increased from three (18.8 percent) to five (20 percent). That progress continued through the next decade. In 2009, women made up only 17 percent of the company's senior leadership. By 2019, 37 percent of the company's senior executive positions were held by women.

Titled "Making Every Day Count: Driving Business Success Through the Employee Experience," Sodexo's approach was to provide the tools, resources, and support necessary to champion the success of all employees, but especially women. "Making Every Day Count" consisted of a series of professional development programs designed to share diversity lessons, provide training to all employees, and develop new professional connections through networking and mentoring, all delivered through Sodexo's eight employee network groups (ENGs). Then the company tied compensation to diversity improvement, with results impacting 10 to 25 percent of senior management bonuses. Clearly, I would love to see more organizations offer financial incentives for upping the percentage of women promoted to achieve gender parity more quickly.

The good news is that Sodexo saw results. The company found that teams with gender-balanced management were 23 percent more likely to see an increase in gross profit. Also, an internal Sodexo study showed that operating margins were 8 percent higher in teams managed by a balanced mix of men and women. Today, Sodexo is woman-led, with Sophie Bellon, the company founder's daughter, having taken over as CEO in early 2022 with full board support. The company is already seeing improvements to its bottom line post-pandemic.

This, once again, materially supports the view that when a company has a practical, conscious, long-term, and results-based plan to close its gender gap at the executive level, the company does better. Just so you don't think these two examples are anomalies, keep reading. I think you will be surprised.

Professional services firm Accenture, which ranks #1 on DiversityInc's 2022 Top 50 list, became the first company in its industry to publish comprehensive data about its US workforce back in 2016. It also has 100 percent dollar-for-dollar pay equity for women versus men in every country in which it operates. In 2017, Accenture committed to a gender-balanced workforce by 2025. As of 2022, it has already taken good strides, with women making up 50 percent of its board of directors and 27 percent of its global management committee. Additionally, 47 percent of its new hires are women, 44 percent of promotions are women, and 32 percent of the firm's executives are women. Part of this progress is because more women are graduating from finance programs with better degrees and higher standing, making them desirable candidates for leading management consulting and accounting firms. Accenture is getting there more quickly than other firms because it put a stake in the ground, invested deliberately, and committed to a gender-balanced workforce.

Medtronic, the global medical device manufacturer, took a similar approach, setting targets for women in leadership roles as a starting point for moving women into more senior positions. Its corporate goal was to have 40 percent or more women in global leadership by 2020. That top line goal then evolved into a 40-30-20 target of 40 percent or more women in global leadership, 30 percent or more women at the manager level or above, and 20 percent or more ethnically diverse managers in the US. As of 2020, Medtronic had achieved percentages of 38-25-22. By 2022, the company continues to produce strong financial results, with revenues of $31 billion and a rising stock price.

One of Medtronic's more unique DEI program elements, which may turn out to be one of its most effective, is its male-targeted daylong "Men Enabling Inclusion" seminars targeted at men. The purpose of the workshop is to help male R&D managers understand the value of inclusion and diversity and how they can help drive positive culture change. However (remember, we said this is an all-in exercise), the one glaring weakness I see is that as of 2020, only 300 R&D leaders across the US had been exposed to and completed the program. I am also curious as to why only US managers were involved when Medtronic is headquartered in Ireland.

And why only a small percentage of its 90,000+ employee base? According to Medtronic, there are more than 11,600 scientists and engineers on its payroll; by my calculation, 300 is just over 2 percent. This will demonstrate the need for focused, determined action. Lastly, where is the accountability for Medtronic's senior executive group and its board of directors?

Best Buy is another enterprise that committed to some very specific programs and practices designed to increase female participation in the higher ranks of the company. In 2017, Best Buy signed Parity.org's ParityPLEDGE, which involves agreeing to interview at least one qualified female candidate for every open position at the vice president level and above. Additionally, the company set its own goal to fill one of every three new, non-hourly field roles with women. With these hiring targets, the company should quickly see results.

On top of relatively new smart hiring-related policies, Best Buy also provides an above-average level of caregiving support, which is aimed at easing the load that women employees need to shoulder. From four paid weeks of caregiving support for family members, to emergency backup childcare, to a personalized caregiving support service, flexible hours, and mental health benefits, Best Buy appears to recognize that the caregiving responsibilities almost always fall on women, which, as we know, can interfere with their ability to advance at work. By introducing caregiving policies and benefits, Best Buy is actively trying to level the playing field.

All of these new corporate policies and practices have been introduced as steps toward achieving gender parity. These companies, and others, are realizing that in order to elevate women in the corporate hierarchy, they need to help them shoulder the personal and caregiving burdens that men are not willing to help with.

If you think, "Yeah, but that wouldn't work in my industry or my corporate sector," you would be wrong. Gender parity works without regard to a specific industry or a sector within an industry. Another reason why this issue continues to confound and exasperate women. Keep reading.

Liberty Mutual seems to have zeroed in on men as the missing link (no pun intended) between employing qualified female employees and moving them up and into more senior positions. The company launched its "Men as Allies" program in 2016 with learning resources and guidance to help men improve their inclusivity and collaboration skills. Ideally, the company hopes to get them on the side of women who need male allies to progress. There was a Men as Allies summit in 2017 and the launch of an intranet and discussion forum for men to discuss "allyship" and all that goes with it. Since then, the company has expanded its notion of allyship to encourage allies within several discreet communities within Liberty Mutual, from Hispanic and Latinx to military veterans, LGBTQ members, Asian employees, differently abled workers, and several other self-identifying groups.

However, when it comes to actual outcomes, we have not seen much progress. I applaud Liberty Mutual for acknowledging the key role men play in vaulting women into more senior jobs, but it appears there has been a lot of talk and not a great deal of action, at least so far. Sure, participants back in 2017 ranked the Men as Allies summit highly for usefulness and were apparently active in the discussion groups then, but as far as helping women make actual progress, we have not yet seen any reports addressing their success on that front to date. The fact that the summit was never repeated and several new allyship initiatives sprang up suggests that Liberty Mutual is perhaps less focused on convincing men like you to help women along than it was mid-decade, or more likely, it continues to struggle to get buy-in from its entrenched male executives in what is typically viewed as an inherently conservative industry sector.

Another professional services firm, PwC, made great strides toward gender equality, moving from a global leadership team that was 20 percent female in 2016 to 38 percent female representation by 2020—a 90 percent increase in four years. To its credit, when PwC discovered the company was "predominantly replacing departing employees with male experienced hires," management immediately tried to put a stop to that by placing a priority on identifying "diverse experienced hires as a critical KPI for global D&I acceleration." To support the promotion of more diverse employees, PwC relied on a new program called "Blind Spots," which was developed to help employees challenge their own assumptions, enhance objectivity, overcome stereotypes, and broaden perspectives.

I suspect what was happening at PwC is what generally happens everywhere—openings created by outgoing employees are routinely filled with men, by men, because the people typically making those decisions are also men, who not so coincidentally surround themselves with other like-minded men. I understand why this happens—it's natural to want the people in your inner circle, who look like you do, whom you know, like, and trust to get the new job. The problem is that few of those people are women because you haven't yet introduced them to your network or treated them as part of your friend group. My takeaway is that you need to interrupt, confront, disrupt, and then figuratively banish this deeply ingrained corporate response and then, with equally deliberate intent, offer openings to more of the highly qualified women who are also in your employ. If you want any chance of a broader market competitive advantage, you will do this now.

The examples I have just shared represent only a sampling of the tactics different corporations in entirely different industry sectors have employed to try to address the lack of women in senior management. There are certainly others, but even within this short list, there are few companies that have found entirely effective ways of encouraging men to hire and promote female employees. That is likely because the central problem originates with the individual—with your male-centric cultural background—rather than a dictated corporate structural model. Your employer likely is not dictating who you should hire or promote—that decision is being left to you. However, when there are long and typically deeply held personal biases and stereotypes in place, it can take massive effort to convince men to re-evaluate those beliefs and then *do something* to counteract the mindset in place. On the other hand, if you are the boss, what is holding you back?

Like Marc Benioff, who saw what needed to be done—he dug in and began to initiate a major corporate sea change at Salesforce. Keep reading.

The First Step Is Acknowledging There Is a Problem

Adjusting CEO mindsets seems to be a big part of this shift toward allyship and support. Marc Benioff, co-CEO of Salesforce, admitted that when two women leaders in the company shared that they believed there was a gender pay gap in some positions within the company, he refused to believe them. Mainly, he says, because he had been working on addressing the clear lack of women leaders in the company since 2012, and he did not want to hear that Salesforce had not made as much progress as he had planned for or had hoped. Acknowledging that they could be right meant that he had not succeeded.

But instead of being defensive, he doubled down and instituted new policies to raise the number of women who were in any management meeting. In his book *Trailblazer*, Benioff shares that one tactic he introduced was to require that "at least 30 percent of the participants at any meeting, from a large management session to a small product review, should be women." (Now, 30 percent is not 50 percent, obviously, but it is certainly a hell of a lot better than the 5 or 10 percent that was closer to the case originally.)

Additionally, in 2015, Salesforce commissioned a pay audit across all levels of the company and discovered that 6 percent of its female workers were being underpaid, *Wired* reported. Those employees were given immediate raises, which totaled $3 million, as a first step toward parity. Benioff took action, for which I applaud him.

In fact, that adjustment was the first of many. To date, the company has completed a total of seven equal pay assessments and spent more than $22 million to address pay disparity.

But a bigger problem, Benioff admits, is the unconscious bias that men are generally unwilling to acknowledge they possess. Yet, in the *Wired* article, Benioff also recounts his "aha" moment. During a 2017 Salesforce event where there were four key speakers, three men and one woman, he shook the hands of the three men and hugged the woman as each took to the stage. It was his wife who pointed out his differing behavior and the fact that he had treated the female speaker less professionally. That realization opened Benioff's eyes and pushed him to continue to build in processes that ensure women receive the same opportunities and pay as their male counterparts, though he admits it is a "recurring problem" that has to be constantly monitored to ensure women are getting what they deserve.

This unconscious bias against women reared its ugly head at my friend Samantha's employer. After about a year in her entry-level job in a small business, she had demonstrated she was ready to be promoted. Her colleagues and one of the two top managers in the company expected her to be moved into a more senior position, but the other manager was adamantly against it. Instead, the other manager moved a more recent male hire to fill a job opening. Samantha was angry and crushed since she had been led to believe the next opening was hers.

She then learned from her peers that the manager was doing all he could to keep her in her current job. He didn't want her progressing and had been complaining to the CEO about her.

Not sure how to handle the situation, Samantha kept doing her best as she tried to figure out whether to stick it out in the hopes something would change or to leave. She wasn't sure what she had done to turn this manager against her. Then, one afternoon, the CEO stopped in and started chatting with Samantha, praising her for her hard work and dedication. She was honestly shocked, unaware that he had even noticed. Turns out, he had, and he had also heard from other employees about what an asset she was.

Samantha admitted quite candidly that she was surprised to hear this since one of the two managers seemed to dislike her. No, the CEO explained, it wasn't that he disliked her; it was that in his culture, women were not viewed as equals. If asked, the manager likely would not have been able to recognize this, but he definitely did not want her to be promoted. He could not conceive of her advancing and perhaps being considered for his role eventually, so he put his foot on her skirt, as it were.

Fortunately, in this situation, the CEO caught wind of what was going on, recognized Samantha's abilities, and demoted her antagonist manager, thus ensuring that Samantha would be promoted. But it is this kind of unconscious bias that, when acted out, is unfairly holding women back. It goes unnoticed at the highest level. However, pressure from various sources is now being applied to businesses to report on progress being made toward gender parity in the workforce.

Government Support for Action

One organization working to push companies to do better by improving diversity is the US government through its EEO report. The Equal Employment Opportunity Compliance report, also known as the EEO-1, is a mandatory annual filing that all private sector companies with one hundred or more employees or federal contractors with fifty or more employees must submit. It includes demographic data on the organizations' workforce, including race or ethnicity, gender, and job category.

While the US government gathers this data and analyzes it, for many years, the results have been kept "under the radar." Few companies have shared their EEO-1 reports with the public. However, pressure from investors and the business community in general has pushed more corporations to share their EEO data. According to *Pensions & Investments*, "Asset owners, interest groups, and employees all want to see whether and how money managers are making progress on diversity—even if the numbers are bad. As such, firms are also being pushed to release more data through a combination of external pressure and new initiatives launched by data compilers and providers." We are already seeing slightly, and I do mean slightly, increased voluntary (and I use the term loosely) disclosure and sharing due to this pressure.

According to Just Capital, an independent research nonprofit that measures and reports on corporate performance, as of December 2019, only thirty-two companies out of 931, or 3.4 percent of companies, publicly reported their diversity data. However, by January 2021, fifty-nine companies, or 6.3 percent of US corporations, were disclosing it. That is an 84 percent increase, although it represents just a very small fraction of the total database of companies. If you're keeping score, that means 872 of these companies are refusing to release their data. These 872 companies know they are falling short regarding diversity and don't want anyone to know it! That's an extraordinary number of companies, and the abysmal results underscore the ongoing nature of the need to address the issue head-on. Even so, we may see the slight uptick in publishing these EEO-1 results as a small sign of hope that corporations will stop trying to bury their poor performance when it comes to diversity, pay equity, and female management hires.

This is where we are in the corporate evolution. Companies have started to recognize the value that women bring to the corporate landscape and the positive impact their presence and contributions have on the bottom line. We also now definitely know that the best starting point for addressing the barriers to progress is sitting at your desk. You, sir, figuratively speaking, and the assumptions you hold that inform the management choices you make may well be the reason companies are feeling compelled to debunk the myths and long-held stereotypes in the way of women's advancement. Unaddressed, men will continue promoting and advancing the people in their immediate circle—meaning, essentially, other men. Companies seeing the greatest improvements are working with men to get them on their side with mentoring. At the same time, the most senior management in these companies is making it known that they are aligning themselves with women within their organizations. Even so, it is clear, given the disappointing results we are still seeing, that there remains significant resistance or pushback to these programs. What other explanation is there for the slow uptake of the re-evaluation of women's value in a corporate setting?

Once again, women need your help to direct or persuade your male colleagues to give the women in your organization a chance. The good news is that your employer wants and will reward your support. It is truly a win-win, if you are willing to try it on.

JUST THE FACTS, SIR.

- White women are expected to receive wage parity, or equal pay to their male counterparts, in the year 2059, according to the Institute for Women's Policy Research, but for Latino women, they won't receive parity with white men until 2206.

- Because of sex discrimination lawsuits filed in the late 1990s and early 2000s costing companies hundreds of millions of dollars in total, new hires on Wall Street are typically required to sign arbitration contracts agreeing not to join class action suits, *Harvard Business Review* reports.

- The year 2021 was the first time more than half of all corporations globally had an anti-sexual harassment policy in place, says Equileap.

- "Between September 2020 and September 2021, the share of companies disclosing an EEO-1 Report or Intersectional Data, the gold standard for demographic data reporting, has more than doubled, from 4 percent to 11 percent," reports JUST Capital.

CHAPTER 8

Just Put One Loafer In Front of the Other and Keep Going

S O, AS IS ALMOST ALWAYS THE CASE, THERE IS SOME GOOD NEWS and some not-so-good news. The good news, of course, is that some companies are starting to take action to support their female employees and proactively help them advance their careers. The not-so-good news is that there are still relatively few companies who are aggressively addressing the issue and, too often, the policies and practices being instituted by those companies on board with the idea of change do not go nearly far enough. The result? Little systemic headway has been made with respect to women's advancement to senior management and corporate leadership.

To varying degrees, some companies have decided that helping women progress professionally is worth doing. Sort of. Some organizations clearly understand the challenge and are going "all in," publicly pledging to do better with new programs, metrics, and financial incentives, all intended primarily to encourage their male employees to do what is right. On the flip side of that coin, those that are not "all in" remain manifestly indifferent. They may proclaim empathy for women and acknowledge how difficult it is to get promoted or reach the most senior management levels, but then they go right back to business as usual. So, solely based on their inaction to date, one can only assume they are not serious and have no real interest in change. I doubt I am misreading their intentions, kind of like the calm before the storm that never comes. What may be an interesting but unexpected outcome for these recalcitrant organizations is that they may notice before too long that they are losing competitive advantage or falling short of industry gains. They may well be inadvertently taking themselves out of the game.

But can you imagine overtly and deliberately impeding progress toward a better business model? We would think that implausible today. However, that is what has been happening in the United Kingdom (UK). Male managers are actively blocking efforts to address gender balance. A 2022 Chartered Management Institute study of 1,149 managers across the UK found that there was passive, and even active, resistance to gender equality from male bosses in many companies: "Two-thirds of male managers believed their organization could successfully manage future challenges without gender-balanced leadership." Instead of progress and improvement, words like "resistance" and "backlash" have been used.

Granted, change is hard and complex. It can be painful, disruptive, uncomfortable, and time-consuming. Yet we have now learned unequivocally that when a policy of gender parity is instituted, change can be tremendous, impressive, satisfying, and, most critically, profitable! That is what I want for you, for us—change that makes you feel good about your company, your work on behalf of women everywhere, and yourself, for your contributions to a new, culturally appropriate corporate order. All of that and a better top and bottom line.

What else can and should be done to give women opportunities to rise in the ranks? I think we need to use both the proverbial carrot and the stick, meaning incentives for results and consequences for shortfalls. Companies should be "educated," and then senior leaders should be incentivized in whatever way a board or an ownership group believes is necessary to effect results. Consider this: It often follows in the corporate realm that if companies cannot or will not adopt change programs or be persuaded to accelerate the necessary rate of change with programs on incentivization and negative consequence for failure, then there exists the real possibility that sooner than one might think, legislation designed to compel change with concomitant regulation to enforce compliance is entirely possible. Why not self-regulate as opposed to exposing yourself and your organization to the often heavy and misdirected hand of government?

Incentives

Assuming organizations want to achieve the best results possible performance-wise, women need to be involved. What follows is a series of positive workplace changes that have been proven to work:

New Paths to Leadership

Twenty years ago, the C-suite consisted primarily of the CEO, CFO, and COO. They were the triumvirate; breaking in was nearly impossible, for men or women. Today, however, several new C-level roles have been created, reflecting the complex world in which we now live and the more complex ways in which business is undertaken. To those three roles, Deloitte reports we are now seeing variations of titles such as Chief Brand, Chief Human Resource, Chief Strategy, Chief Innovation, Chief Diversity and Inclusion, Chief Privacy, Chief Sustainability, and Chief Data Officer. They also report that women are having more success at landing these newly created positions. According to Deloitte, in 2019, women held 32.5 percent of those emerging C-suite roles versus 27 percent of the old three more traditional Chief Officer roles.

Why is that though? Deloitte wondered too and surmised that "it is possible that emerging roles are unencumbered by the obstacles that have historically impeded women's journey to leadership. What is more, many of these roles—frequently hybrids—tend NOT to have a set career path, which could result in more avenues to reach them."

In fact, women currently hold the majority of chief human resource officer (CHRO) roles, according to HR Dive. This one may not be so shocking because, as I've stated many times earlier, this is typically considered a "women's job." I think the difference is that making this a C-suite position gives the jobholder more power and more say in the running of the company. "Women in CHRO roles at companies in the Equilar 500—the information services firm's list of the 500 largest companies trading on major US stock exchanges—both outnumber and outearn their male counterparts." The percent of women who have held the CHRO title in the Equilar 500 has risen steadily, from 42 percent in 2017 to 59 percent in 2020, and to 75 percent in 2021. Perhaps a more salient fact is that female CHROs in the Equilar 500 earned a median pay of $3 million versus the median pay for men at $1.6 million. This is progress!

At the same time, it points out the glaring disparity that can find its way into corporate structures for no apparent set of causes or reasons. Are we now saying men are being paid less because their contributions in this specific corporate stream can't be valued as women's might be based on some imputed gender differential? Surely not.

That said, we now have former human resource leaders who have risen into the CEO spot: Mary Barra at General Motors, who was formerly vice president of global human resources at GM, and Chanel Global CEO Leena Nair, who was formerly CHRO at Unilever, are two big success stories. They are blazing new pathways to senior leader roles.

I think the lesson that we can draw from this discussion is that by creating new positions with elevated titles at the highest levels, the path up and ahead for women in those roles opens wider. There are more opportunities for growth and advancement for everyone, but from my perspective, women will have a greater chance at qualifying for these new and now essential chief officer positions since there is not the long-standing and entrenched career ladder embedded in corporate structure as there is with the traditional CEO, CFO, and COO positions.

What I said before about board positions holds true here. If there are not enough spots for women, create new ones; enlarge the circle to make space. Smart companies are doing exactly that.

Advanced Analytics and Artificial Intelligence (AI)

We are talking now about improving the quality of the core data that might be used to measure progress within an organization. Although we are seeing increased attention to DEI initiatives, which is a move in the right direction, the data being examined is not necessarily complete or correct. It follows that reliance on that data can lead to faulty assumptions and strategies for closing the gender gap when it comes to career progression.

Many corporations rely on data from their EEO-1 report to guide decision-making, sometimes to the exclusion of other sources and resources. However, more experts are realizing that such an approach is incomplete and perhaps even faulty. The EEO-1 report does not really allow for broader contextual interpretation and can lead readers to perceive progress that quite simply is not there. Today, the use of advanced analytics can shine a spotlight on data elements that have so far remained hidden or obscured. Without advanced analytics, the analysis of an EEO-1 report is akin to assuming that you can make a twenty-foot putt with your eyes closed. Please, do not misunderstand me, the EEO-1 is an important document and should still be made available to all employees, but it's just one tool in the toolbox upon which to base policy changes. Analytics are another such tool.

IBM actually began to question this reliance on EEO-1 data and published its 2021 report, "Women, Leadership, and Missed Opportunities," to share what had been learned. A key finding was:

> "Few companies would dream of launching a major product initiative without pulling in their best data, analytics, and talent. But some organizations rely on conventional wisdom to guide gender and inclusion initiatives. They choose interventions because of reputations for good practice without testing whether these 'done before' efforts are the best route to deliver desired outcomes—or whether alternative approaches might generate better results."

The point is simply that if companies invest more time in analyzing all of the internal data they have access to and couple it with market and industry data, it is highly likely they will uncover new paths to improvement. Tapping into the power of artificial intelligence (AI) to identify patterns or takeaways from what they have in front of them is sure to lead to new ideas for promoting women, given what the data will show is that businesses achieving gender parity are already yielding positive results.

Years ago, when I first started to speak publicly about the lack of advancement of women in leadership roles, I challenged my audiences to go back to their organizations and just start counting. Simply count the number of women at every level of the organization. I cannot tell you how many folks came back to me and admitted that until they did that one fundamental but simple thing, they had not realized to what a significant extent their organizations were lacking in gender parity.

Destigmatize Flexible Work

Another opportunity exists for companies willing to build in more flexibility around work for all employees. We all know that women routinely shoulder multiple roles and certainly more than most men. Women's roles often include being, simultaneously, a spouse or partner, mother, daughter, sister, maid, cook, nanny, chauffeur, concierge, financial manager, and volunteer, in addition to being an employee, breadwinner, or entrepreneurial employer. Women have become expert jugglers of tasks and excellent managers of time, essentially out of necessity.

The recent pandemic shone a spotlight on the overwhelming burden of all those roles, and many employers, in response, recognized that they needed to offer more flexibility with respect to their working arrangements. This is more often an issue that significantly impacts the choices women can make, given the multiplicity of roles they are compelled to play. This point was made clear at insurance firm Zurich when it witnessed the number of women applying for management roles jump by nearly 20 percent after the company included words like "part-time," "job share," and "flexible working" in its employment ads. Women need more flexibility when so many other family-related tasks are a part of every day, not just the conventional eight-hour workday.

To recast the view that it is only women who need the flexibility, men could and should begin to take advantage of these options. All men should support *and* take advantage of the option for flexible hours when it is available, especially if you are a parent or caregiver in some capacity. Use your vacation time. Take advantage of your employment benefits like paternity leave, actively contribute at home, and in doing so, you will help to reduce any of the lingering gender-based stigma attached to women using the maternity leave they need and deserve.

Parental Leave

Speaking of parental leave, companies should make parental leave—meaning for women and men—on the birth or adoption of their child a company-wide policy. Companies should consider the possibility of making some form of paternal leave mandatory. The United States is unusual, and except for a few states, some would say far behind most of the contemporary corporate world globally in not mandating or incentivizing paid parental leave for all new parents. In the US, larger employers are required to make available twelve weeks of unpaid leave. This is not a solution. Firstly, it is not required that the employee use the mandated leave, and secondly, because it is often unpaid, not all employees can afford to stay home. The absence of the paycheck is a huge and very predictable disincentive. It is "false progress." It virtually ensures a very limited subset of the population can generally take advantage of this option, these being women: women who can afford to take time off while foregoing income.

Moreover, while the law prohibits companies from replacing women while they are out on maternity leave, that does not mean they are not disadvantaged. Being out of the corporate loop for several months can, and often does, impact their career trajectory on their return, which often in turn impacts the likelihood of future promotions. Some women deliberately choose to step down to the "mommy track," which means they are not looking for the frequent promotions that other more ambitious women aspire to. Others are unknowingly relegated to the "mommy track" by their employers, who make unfounded assumptions about their motivation to have a child and draw erroneous conclusions about their priorities once they have children. This is particularly galling when, on their return to work, those female employees demonstrate quickly that they are just as committed to their jobs and as ambitious about advancement as they were immediately before they took a maternity leave. This is both unfair to the employee and, as we have seen, potentially a costly false assumption by the employer.

According to *Fast Company*, "The best leaders today are caregivers, yet we are losing our best leaders to caregiving. If we encourage all new parents to take parental leave and share the responsibility at home, we will create equal opportunity in the workplace and caregiving will not be the primary responsibility of women." I would add to that conclusion that, were that to happen, it may bring an end to the gender-specific implications that now only negatively impact women.

Gentlemen, as fathers, it is important for you to take parental leave. Your child needs to bond with you differently, but equally, as much as with their mother. Parenting is difficult enough without the majority of parental responsibilities being allocated to the mother. You need to completely understand how exhausting it is to have a newborn in the house. If you are not there, you have no way of knowing the number of feedings, multiple wailing sessions, the amount of laundry, the amount of havoc one small newborn can generate in a twenty-four-hour day. Changing a couple of diapers when you get home from work and maybe giving the baby a bottle or two is not the same thing as being around the baby 24/7. Parenting needs to be shared and tasks and responsibilities need to be equally divided. Family or parental leave should not be considered a perk; it is not a luxury, it is a necessity—for both a mother and a father. Corporations need to acknowledge and accept that as a fact. Men must share the responsibility. Get your family started and then both get back to work without fear of penalty or career consequence.

Childcare Infrastructure

Once back from parental leave, regardless of whether these new mothers have had a spouse or partner supporting them at home, an employer should expect to face an additional challenge, namely, how to hold onto valued women employees who may be adjusting to juggling all of those earlier described elements they have been responsible for, and now a newborn. At a minimum, know this: They will be exhausted! Remember, they don't get sleep during the night yet, and with this added responsibility of caring for a child, or possibly other children, a woman sometimes makes a very hard choice, intellectually, emotionally, and financially, and simply opts to drop out of the workforce altogether. This is not good for anyone, really, least of all you as her employer. Finding a replacement, educating and training, and then empowering are all a part of the very expensive churn process that does not have to happen. However, without adequate and appropriate support on returning to the workplace, it is often too much of an adjustment. It is very much worth noting that, seven or eight months into the pandemic, more than 800,000 women left the workforce between August and September 2020 alone, according to the *New York Times*. The reasons: simple and complicated at the same time.

Having to manage work, childcare, and remote schooling became too difficult for some women, and understandably so. *Harvard Business Review* estimates that women perform 2.5 times the amount of unpaid labor as men. As an aside, and only somewhat tongue-in-cheek, I think perhaps men came up with that estimate because it sounds woefully low based on what I have personally experienced and witnessed.

Of course, this "gender responsibility imbalance," as I call it, which persists today, also represents a real opportunity for companies that are willing to invest in childcare infrastructure in support of the women who work for them. By childcare infrastructure, I am talking about introducing policies and benefits to ease the burden on mothers, such as:

- Flexible or remote work
- Unlimited vacation (take what you need and could be a combination of paid and unpaid)
- Pay equality
- Benefits for schooling or tutoring
- Childcare subsidy (to include cost of daycare or in-home help)
- Corporate in-house childcare
- Babysitting coverage for after-hour commitments
- Mental health support

Without adequate support at work, women may exit the workforce, sometimes temporarily and sometimes for as long as their children are at home. The *Washington Post* looked into why women did not return to the workforce in droves once schools returned to in-person instruction in 2022, during the COVID era, and found "that in states where childcare is more affordable and more easily accessible, and where federal and state programs are more generous, mothers are more likely to be employed." And conversely, in states where childcare is less affordable, going back to work may not make economic sense for some women. They may want to, but they may not be able to afford to. The US Census estimates that of the 10.5 million single-parent households, 7.8 million are headed by women. That should be a sobering statistic for you.

Companies willing to invest in programs that support women and their roles as parent and caregiver help them stay on the career path and advance. I believe it follows that this should simply be viewed as just another form of investment that the employer will benefit from.

However, not all companies are willing to entertain any of the ideas put forth here. Many are not interested in investing in benefits to recruit and retain female employees, and they are unlikely to make any accommodations or exceptions for those they already employ. They erroneously believe or, more likely, adopt as a convenient rationalization that equality means no gender differentiation on the playing field of the corporation, which, of course, perpetuates a playing field that is clearly not level. It is these organizations that may need a different kind of helping hand to get with the program. We may well need to consider a stick when the carrot does not work.

I recently spoke with a friend who works for a large insurance company whose executives (mostly male) take great pride in talking about the new headquarters building they had just moved into. It *was* state-of-the-art. Full marks. With all the mod-cons. It had an amazing gym, a hoteling design concept to accommodate remote workers, e-offices, meeting areas, and break rooms with vivid colors and furnishings. They even provided a bar with wine and beer on tap. Every employee was provided a pass card that allowed them to swipe and access a number of alcoholic drinks a day each. Everyone thought it was very progressive. The intent was to provide a place for all levels of employees to chat over a beverage after work hours—to provide an opportunity to create relationships and increase collaboration.

The addition of the bar was concerning to my friend, so she suggested that perhaps a better idea would be to consider transforming that space into a daycare, given that 70 percent of the company's workforce was women—and mostly women who were mothers who had to shuttle their kids to and from daycare every day. The immediate but no less baffling response was that a daycare would not only be costly to set up, it would pose significant liability issues. She assumed someone calculated the liability risk of providing free alcohol to employees in a work setting and then allowing them to drive home. One can probably imagine who hung out in the bar regularly. Full credit if you guessed it wasn't the moms rushing to pick up kids and get home for dinner with them. This story leaves me speechless...a rare event, as most who know me would tell you.

Mandates

Over many decades, beginning in the late 1930s, recognizing the value and importance of supporting women in the workforce, and mindful of the need to eradicate the discrimination and sexism that runs rampant, the US government has introduced various pieces of legislation setting threshold standards that corporations were obliged to meet to help women progress. This legislative process started back in 1938 with the Fair Labor Standards Act, which was an attempt to ensure women could earn a living wage, followed by the Equal Pay Act, Title VII (prohibiting wage discrimination based on gender), the Pregnancy Discrimination Act, and the Family and Medical Leave Act, all of which were written and passed in an effort to prohibit companies from discriminating against women in the workplace. Over the years, some states have taken additional steps to even the playing field, such as with California's SB 826, a 2018 state law requiring the 717 publicly held companies based in the state to have at least one woman on its corporate boards. Although that law has recently been struck down (and inexplicably not re-introduced as of yet in a different form), while the legislation was in force, California's efforts did make great headway—99.3 percent of companies had met the requirement before the deadline. My expectation is that, even in the absence of the ongoing enforcing legislation, those women who did get board seats are having an impact and clearing the way for more women. I do know they will not go quietly but rather will pull and push until more progress has been made. I comment below on the history of that legislation in California and fervently hope legislation like it is advanced in many other state legislatures in the near future.

Additionally, outside interest groups are also applying pressure in various ways, including investors who are beginning to engage in "values-based" enterprise investments and not simply "dollar" value-based companies. The intent is that companies will change their attitude and will decide to encourage, rather than discourage, the women on their payrolls.

Board Representation

As referred to above, the state of California took center stage with its efforts to improve gender equality in the workplace by requiring greater diversity on corporate boards. Championed by Betsy Berkhemer-Credaire, CEO and owner of Berkhemer Clayton Inc., a premier executive search firm committed to increasing gender and ethnic diversity at the C-suite and boardroom corporate levels. Betsy led the successful campaign to secure passage of SB 826 in California, effective January 2019, the first and only law in the US requiring every public company in California to have at least three women board members before year-end 2021. Unfortunately, two years later, in 2020, California lawmakers added new requirements, including that California corporations must have one director from an underrepresented community by year-end 2021, with other requirements by year-end 2022. Penalties for failing to reach these representation percentages were fines of between $100,000 and $300,000 per violation.

Unfortunately, there was what might have been unexpected, but what was clearly predictable, backlash against this legislation, led by nonprofit conservative advocacy group Judicial Watch, and in April 2022, the state court ruled the mandates unconstitutional because quotas were stipulated and struck down the law. Questions now remain about the next steps to ensure diversity on corporate boards in that state and in others.

Investor Pressures

As stated earlier, investors have been exerting pressure and now, at a board governance level, large institutional investors are demanding more board representation from their corporate holdings. They are leveraging their ownership stakes to try to force companies to make progress. *Kellogg Insight* reported that "the Big Three" are making more headway in this regard than government legislation. Researchers observed:

"...the conspicuous uptick in female directorships coincided with a cascade of gender-diversity influence campaigns mounted by a trio of powerful institutional investors: Vanguard, BlackRock, and State Street. Known as 'the Big Three,' these firms manage over $15 trillion, accounting for three-quarters of indexed mutual fund assets. That means that these companies hold shares in almost every large firm in the US—in fact, they are the *dominant* shareholder in 88 percent of firms on the S&P 500."

Apparently, when the Big Three tells you to up the number of women on your board, you do it.

Researchers estimated that the Big Three's campaigns led firms to add at least 2.5 times as many female directors in 2019 as they had in 2016, accounting for most of the increase in board gender diversity over that period.

Following gender diversity ad campaigns in 2017, the researchers found, "Each member of the Big Three also backed up its campaign with a threat: it would vote against directors at any firms who failed to appoint more women to their boards. Directors on a corporate board are elected by the firm's shareholders." And then they closely monitored the moves their holdings made over the next year with respect to board composition.

Reported the researchers, "The results were undeniable: the more of a firm's stock the Big Three held, the more women directors appeared on that firm's board after 2017." The veiled threats worked. Progress was miraculously made, if slowly and begrudgingly made.

For every additional 8 percent owned by Vanguard, BlackRock, or State Street, the number of new female board members rose by 76 percent. Before 2017, only one in twelve firms added a woman to its board each year. By 2019, one in four did.

While it is much easier to impress upon someone the importance of making a certain decision when you have leverage, sometimes the key to change is removing that leverage, or that information. Such as in the case of salary information.

Salary History Ban

While it is much easier to bring about a desired result when you have leverage, sometimes the key to change is removing the element that is giving one group (employers) leverage over another (potential women employees). Such is the case with information concerning salary or wages. For decades, job candidates have been asked to share their current salary with potential employers. This has become one more piece of information that companies can use to decide whether to hire someone and what starting salary to offer. Inferring that someone's salary reflects their performance and capabilities is both incorrect and prejudicial. Given that women statistically earn less than men almost across the board, demanding that female job candidates report their current salary only serves to help potential employers continue to keep them on the lower pay path they are currently on rather than bumping up their compensation to match their talent, education, title, and intended responsibilities. Ignoring past salary information and paying women what they are worth, or what other male colleagues are earning for the same work, is the only path to ultimately establishing corporate pay equity.

This is why we need to stop asking job applicants the question about their current salary and other forms of compensation altogether. What applicants are currently earning should have no bearing on what they are paid in the future at a new job. To date, twenty-one states have agreed and have instituted legislative or regulatory bans on requiring pay history to be considered for job applicants. Only twenty-one states. We still have a long way to go.

A better recruitment approach for a company to take would be for an employer to publish salary ranges for a job vacancy or new position that is to be filled and then use that information as the basis for salary discussions with job candidates, without demanding information about what the candidate currently earns. (See the discussion that follows under "Pay Transparency.") That information should be irrelevant. When demanded by a potential employer, it has historically been a device keeping women from making what their male counterparts are earning. The employment marketplace needs to rid itself of policies and practices that expose women to an unnecessary gender bias disadvantage.

Pay Transparency

As a corollary of the above, while the prohibition against requiring current pay information from candidates is gaining ground, pay transparency remains a darker side of the coin. Companies in a small but growing number of states are required to tell job applicants what the job pays. This is a good thing. Not only does it help prevent paying women less than men, it helps all candidates ask for what they believe they are worth. Companies that do not comply with these state laws or regulations can be fined or otherwise censured.

Consider this perspective: If you are transparent about the pay range for a job you are trying to fill, you can comfortably assume the applicant pool will be self-limiting. People do not generally apply for positions at a lower pay grade. You can expect that if a woman applies for a job at a posted salary and benefit rate, she is clearly interested in the job at that pay scale. Now you still need to determine whether her qualifications meet your expectations, but I suggest it is a much better way to separate the wheat from the chaff. Even though men will automatically rate themselves up, a professional HR interviewer comparing women and men candidates for a position at that salary level will quickly be able to differentiate qualifications and personal attributes. This does help level the playing field once again in a way that mitigates as much to the benefit of the employer as it does the prospective employee.

Unfortunately, however, there are differences from state to state as to when applicants must be told what a particular job pays, however. Depending on the state, candidates may receive this information after they submit a formal application, or only when they request it, or after they have been offered the job, or some variation on those timeframes. So, we are not seeing many companies posting what the job pays when they advertise an opening—yet. But I think that time is coming, and it will be good for all employees to know in advance what a job pays. It will also make it more difficult for companies to compensate women and men differently for performing the same job or role in a company.

This same transparency needs to be applied across more of the corporate policies and practices as they emerge. Transparency is valuable for women, just as it is for men. Transparency should benefit the employer and employee. Leveling the playing field requires more open access to more information, and this is valuable for everyone: women, men, and the company.

But once again, none of this can happen unless you agree to help. Having one cheerleader or champion within the organization isn't enough. We need multiple people jumping on the bandwagon if we want real change to happen. I hope, like Professor Randall Peterson of the London Business School, you will agree with him when he said championing change for women at work "only happens when lots of people work hard at it. And I want to be one of those people."

Be like Professor Peterson.

JUST THE FACTS, SIR.

- A recent study found that while women make up about 25 percent of all Fortune 500 CEOs, they only own 1 percent of the value of the aggregate stock shares all the CEOs own. Said another way, men in that group own ninety-nine times more corporate stock than the women CEOs do.

- In Thailand, nearly 12 percent of CEOs in public companies are women, 18 percent are directors, and in the public and private sectors combined, the numbers are anywhere between 30 and 40 percent.

- Research conducted by Ernst & Young reported that "two-thirds of our study participants conclude that the legacy C-suite model is not well-suited to the imperatives of the next decade." Changes need to be made to adequately address coming challenges.

CHAPTER 9

OK Guys, This is It. This is Where
the Rubber Meets the Road

NOW THAT YOU HAVE HEARD FIRSTHAND WHAT WOMEN ROUTINELY encounter and endure at work, and you have learned how some men are consciously and deliberately willfully holding them back from career advancement, can I ask: Are you ready to help? Are you willing to provide support for our progress? You really have nothing to lose here. Helping women advance won't hold you back or slow your own progress. In fact, as we have seen in study after study after study, helping women advance in the workplace allows women to contribute as we have seen they can, and that contribution materially improves results at your company. As has also been demonstrated time and again in the organization, this kind of progress is good for everyone, and that includes you.

It is also the right thing to do for all women. Your wives, your partners, your daughters, and your sisters. All women who need to, want to, and hope to aspire to a rightful place in the corporate world you live in.

You agree with me that there is a problem, and you have seen here that there is a solution, a simple solution. You need to actively intervene to help women make progress. You need to proactively change policies on gender diversification, pay equity, and collateral benefits to allow women to realize their full potential so you gain access to the myriad benefits you and your organization will accrue by doing so.

Conversely, even acknowledging we need your help, if you are unwilling to give it, we will find workarounds, as we have always done. It is not entirely personal, but business is business, and now that we see a solution supported by incontrovertible data confirming the essential value of elevating women to senior roles in the workplace, you're either with us or you're against us. We'd much rather have you with us, of course.

Male-dominated hierarchies have historically defined and controlled the growth of many institutions within our society, so it is no shock that men want to retain that control. Giving women workplace equality, being prepared to share power, means accepting that you will be obliged to give up some element of the power you now hold. It's unnerving, maybe even anxiety-producing, to contemplate ceding control you have long claimed absolute ownership of. Long gone are the days when men needed only to snap their fingers and women would do their bidding, at home, in the classroom, and most assuredly, in the workplace. Now she will leave you, she will report you, she will sue you, and she will cost you your job.

We are not going back to that time, no matter how much some of you would like us to. It is not going to happen. Society has evolved and social economics have been significantly altered. But more importantly, women's ambitions and sense of empowerment have once again been rekindled. And that is colliding with the stubborn resistance of a dwindling group of powerful men. Yes, you are powerful, but the world continues to change in ways that cannot sustain your comfortable status quo. Some of you have moved on and ahead, keeping pace with the changing times. Good on you and well done. Some, on the other hand, would rather die in their tracks, and they just may. But that said, I think all of you in this latter group know it will not be easy going for much longer.

We Are at a Tipping Point

A new world is emerging where women will have a voice—where women will participate in decision-making, problem-solving, and creating new opportunities. Men who refuse to acknowledge them or their ideas will be left behind. We are already seeing that happen, as companies with women serving on the board of directors or leading from the C-suite are producing better results than companies that are still entirely male-centric and thus male-dominated. Soon corporations that have embraced the new gender reality will put the companies unwilling to embrace change in their rearview mirror. Male-dominated companies will get left behind, absorbed, or will be at risk of fiscal malaise, if not outright failure.

We need change. That change will be fueled by understanding or, alternatively, by anger and disappointment. Now that women are more educated, better informed, have experienced firsthand the inequality inherent in our situation and now clearly understand the dynamics of our current state, we are angry about, disappointed in, and determined to change this current state of affairs.

The Start of a Social Movement

Women are frequently catalysts for change, after all. I cannot help but think of the suffragettes who changed the nature of women's voting rights. And Rosie the Riveter—the well-known cultural icon who represented the women working in the factories during World War II who filled in for the male workers while the latter were serving in the military. What may be lost today is that Rosie inspired a social movement that increased the number of working American women by 57 percent in four years. (Granted, these women workers earned just over half of what their male counterparts did when they did the same jobs, but there was a wellspring of support for women continuing to work in Western economies after the Second World War, thanks to Rosie.)

I think it may be appropriate to use this inimitable cultural icon Rosie, once again, but this time perhaps as a symbol of a new fiscal feminism based solely on women's economic power. With these recent tectonic social shifts in women's levels of education, financial independence, and attitudes toward childbearing and rearing, it is becoming increasingly apparent we know that We Can Do It! That is true whether we have your help and support or not, though, of course, we would make faster progress if you were with us. That is why we are sharing all of this information with you now, to alert you that the next inevitable moment of change is afoot and to enlist your participation as we move to accelerate the process.

Join me now in imagining a new corporate world order where at least half of senior leadership positions are in the hands of women, heralding a new and distinctive period of our time in which we all acknowledge, honor, reward, and take advantage of women's extraordinary strengths moving forward.

A Pressing Need for Change

We know that the push for change has been on the horizon and, in some cases, is already here, buoyed by DEI policies that organizations are now voluntarily adopting, grudgingly, in compliance with legislation. DEI policies are making their way to the boardroom and into management value statements and principles as a reflection of what employees, consumers, investors, and governments want. I think, perhaps on some level, we are culturally tired of the same old sexism, racism, and misogyny. At least I'd like to think so.

As part of engaging in the understanding of and the implementation of DEI programs, companies need to start by embracing the concept that diversity and inclusion are the cornerstones of high organizational performance—where all individuals are treated with respect and dignity. Importantly, a new era where all organizational contributions and business decisions are made after considering the perspectives of both women and men. Companies that adopt DEI constructs to develop actionable, practical, and trackable policies and practices really are the ones seeing results.

Making the Commitment

Perhaps the most important aspect of the adoption and implementation of DEI policies and other programs intended to create equity is commitment. Published, clearly stated commitments are tools for accountability. By publishing a commitment to certain policies, everyone who hears of your goals and intentions can help hold you accountable to that commitment or pledge. This is true whether you make a personal pledge or are speaking on behalf of an organization. It is the equivalent of planting a flag in the ground and stating your intentions publicly for all to witness.

So, that is what we need you to do now—pledge your willingness and intention to move women into leadership roles throughout your organization.

However, a pledge by itself is more likely to degrade into wishful thinking. Even if presented as a goal, that is not helpful. We have had too many promises of progress without any accountability for the lack of it. We need a pledge with a published program, clearly identified timelines and milestones, or measurable threshold expectations.

We need you to pledge to advance gender parity in your organization's leadership roles within a certain time frame and to a certain percentage, such as 30 percent within three years and 50 percent within five years, for example. Along with that pledge, perhaps the next step could be the development of a gender parity certification model, not unlike women-owned and minority-owned business certifications, that corporations would be required to meet or achieve to maintain their legal corporate status. If small businesses must jump through hoops to prove they are owned by women, BIPOC citizens, or veterans, why not expect the same level of accountability from larger corporations claiming to be working toward gender parity? Think about that. Wouldn't that drive a significant change in corporate structure?

This is not exactly a novel idea. As of this writing, pledges have been demonstrated to bring about real change in other areas, including climate change, opposition to the war in Ukraine, and support for the Black Lives Matter movement. The Climate Pledge, which more than 300 companies have now signed, signals a corporation's commitment to introducing policies and practices designed to reduce greenhouse gases connected to climate change. When Russia invaded Ukraine, many companies committed to suspending business operations or pulling out of Russia completely in protest. And companies that committed to taking action and donating money in support of the Black Lives Matter movement spurred other organizations to voice their support. These pledges sparked momentum that resulted in policy change and corporate action that spread well beyond select corporations.

Research has shown that true corporate change requires a movement, and movements often start with framing the issue as a first step. In addressing this set of issues, a Women's Corporate Bill of Rights governing the corporation's engagement with its workforce would, in this case, be a powerful way to frame the issue of gender diversity, equity, and inclusion.

It is time to consider committing to a Women's Corporate Bill of Rights. This list of basic rights and privileges could be seen as a type of pledge made by employers, only deeper and stronger. A study of the extent of the use and effectiveness of corporate pledges conducted by *Forbes* found they can lead to action by inspiring accountability. The authors report that:

> "If organizations or countries take public pledges, it is much more likely that employees, customers, residents or citizens will hold that entity accountable for changes, particularly when the top leader or leaders were involved with or agreed to the pledge. This is basic change management."

Pledges are effective catalysts for change. Do you not want to be part of that process and become the driver of an engine for long overdue and inevitable change?

We know that committing resources to a singular goal does make a difference. Look at how nearly every Fortune 500 company jumped on the quality bandwagon. Once the Malcolm Baldrige National Quality Award for process improvement was established in 1987, massive budgets were established to pursue this new honor. Dozens of corporate mission and vision statements were revised to reflect their new commitment to quality. There were quarterly targets set for process improvements and regular executive meetings in many companies to discuss the companies' efforts toward winning that prestigious award.

Although there are only three Baldrige awards given in six total categories each year, it seemed that the vast majority of corporations in nearly every industry were now committed to performance excellence. And while only a few companies earned that distinction each year, quality standards improved across the board. How could they not, with each organization seemingly working almost single-mindedly toward quality improvement?

Women are asking for the same level of commitment and enthusiasm we saw around quality to be applied to gender parity in the workplace.

To say it one last time, with feeling, simply broadly and vaguely pledging to improve your company's record on gender diversity is so broadly shallow and tentative as to be rendered noncommittal if the pledge does not contain specific performance criteria. What, exactly, will your company do to improve gender diversity and equity within the organization? What are some metrics and milestones you will use to gauge your progress? What can women expect from your company in terms of treatment and opportunities? What are women's rights as employees and, more specifically, as female employees? Spell it out.

Some elements I believe should be inalienable rights for all women in all workplaces include the following, which we will call here a "Women's Corporate Bill of Rights."

Women's Corporate Bill of Rights

In my world, the Women's Corporate Bill of Rights guarantees:

- **Equity.** An equal number of women will be given seats at the executive *and* board tables. This will include 50 percent of the educationally or experientially qualified women employees in entry-level and mid-management positions.

- **Priority in advancement.** Promoting women shall be deemed a priority until such time as parity is reached company-wide, with internal promotions of women employees having priority over outside hires. Should outside hires be necessary, women candidates shall have priority until parity is reached.

- **Family-friendly policy enforcement.** It shall be company policy that women will not be discriminated against or arbitrarily held back from career advancement should they choose to have children; *parental leave will be respected as part of a new corporate cultural imperative.*

- **New corporate performance metrics.** Revised metrics of corporate performance that, in addition to ROI or ROA, includes performance improvement on gender parity and equity policies, as well as consumer and employee awareness of specific DEI related programs and initiatives.

- **Formal mentoring program.** A mentoring program shall be instituted whereby all senior executives shall mentor two interested female employees at any employee level for a period of at least six months.

- **Formal executive sponsor program.** Every woman aspiring to a senior leadership role will be assigned an Executive Sponsor.

- **Recognizing and valuing emotional intelligence skills.** Leadership job postings and Ideal Candidate Profiles should include emotional intelligence and empathy skills, not just traditional business attributes, such as statistics, economics, analytics, and accounting.

- **Concise job descriptions.** All job descriptions will be clear, concise, and complete.

- **Objective promotion criteria.** Written, clear, and objective criteria for promotions and salary increases, which are gender-neutral, will be published.

- **Eliminate age-related inquiries.** All job applications will be anonymized and scrubbed of any age-related information, from the position of receptionist to C-suite jobs. If you cannot tell in the interview of qualified candidates, you shouldn't be asking. The object is to eliminate exclusion from the interview process on the basis of declared age alone.

- **Vendor/Business Partner screening and qualification.** To ensure the entities your company does business with have similar values and a call to action to create gender parity, a screening process should be instituted to qualify them on the basis of your company's stated DEI policies and corporate values. Create a waterfall effect through your actions by engaging with others outside your organization.

- **Monthly parity meetings.** Monthly *executive* meetings shall be scheduled to specifically discuss equity and parity in the company, with women of all work levels encouraged to attend and be heard.

- **Professional development plans.** Individual development plans will be created (*a collaboration of* executive, HR, and women employees) to discuss practical ways of helping women employees move into executive positions.

- **Transparency regarding gender diversity statistics.** The EEO-1 report, prepared by all companies required to gather this data under legislation, will be made available to all employees without redaction.

- **Gender-neutral dress code.** All dress codes will be gender-neutral for all employees. No more requiring women to wear skirts or pantyhose while men can wear damn well whatever they want.

- **Gender equality becomes part of purpose.** Gender equality and gender parity will be part of your company's mission statement and brand manifesto.

This may not be a comprehensive list. There may be other principles that are relevant to your organization's specific construct that you may consider adding or the commitments that your employees are requesting, if not demanding, you make. And other pledges that will emerge in the years to come. But at least start with this.

Of course, there are several other women's bills of rights that have been introduced in an effort to shine a spotlight on the struggles that women face in the workplace. There is the Working Woman's Bill of Rights from Legal Momentum, the Workplace Bill of Rights from the nonprofit Workplace Fairness, and even the 1968 Bill of Rights from the National Organization for Women. These are all valiant efforts to bring attention to the need to give women in the workplace their due, but they haven't gotten us anywhere close to where we need to be.

Perhaps previous bills of rights were too far-reaching, trying to do too much? Or maybe they were ahead of their time, as men were still adjusting to women in the workplace? Either way, they were, and clearly remain, insufficient. We need a current and substantive bill of rights that companies commit to upholding: one that women can point to as evidence of what they have been promised by their employers. It's time.

We Are in a New Era

Although company leaders are generally reluctant to stick their necks out in support of or in opposition to anything controversial, the tide is turning. Research conducted at the World Economic Forum in 2022 found that "the proportion of consumers who want companies to take a stand on issues such as sustainability, transparency, or fair employment practice has risen from 62 percent in 2018 to 72 percent in 2022." Your customer base wants to see that you are keeping pace with the way they experience the world, not the way you might wish it were. They want to know that on issues of gender, race, pay equity, and sustainability, you are on their side.

With the world changing at such a rapid rate, too many still cling to our male-contrived, male-dominated hierarchies. It is interesting but sad that even as we begin to recognize women's rights, we continue to fail to recognize their strengths, to credit their capacity to contribute materially to corporate health and wealth! How do we know this? Again, a 2022 World Economic Forum report found that if we continue to let things evolve at the current rate—meaning little noticeable progress—it will likely take 135 years to achieve gender parity. That is several generations into the future. We all, but in particular, men, cannot afford to wait anywhere near that long. Why in God's name would you? Why would you leave all that money and goodwill on the table? So, step up and commit your support for gender parity.

JUST THE FACTS, SIR.

- Says the *Harvard Business Review*, "A high proportion of stakeholders—86 percent on the 2021 Edelman Trust Barometer—believe that business executives must play a lead role in tackling societal issues."

- The American Society of Training and Development (ASTD) did a study of accountability and found that people have a 65 percent likelihood of achieving a goal if they share it first with someone else. That success percentage increases to 95 percent if he or she schedules an accountability appointment with that person to report on their success. Making a pledge public almost guarantees success.

- Machiavelli said, "It must be considered that there is nothing more difficult to carry out, nor more doubtful of success, nor more dangerous to handle, than to initiate a new order of things."

CHAPTER 10

You Read About It, Now Do It

HOPEFULLY, YOU'VE READ THIS ENTIRE BOOK AND REALLY TOOK some time to think about the concepts I have presented to you. So, here's the deal: I know I've been hammering home how you guys are the problem when it comes to gender equality in the workplace—and that is a fact, for the most part—but that is not the entire story. Women must make some changes, too. We need to become aggressively and directly engaged in making change occur.

As I was researching to write this book, even I, who has been banging away at this issue for decades, was struck by just how stark and damning a picture the newer data painted. The data shows us just how deeply embedded the male behaviors at the heart of gender imbalance have been. It is its own kind of catastrophe, a tragedy played out on a much grander scale for much longer than what we typically think of as constituting a catastrophe. But you guys really need to see the value in helping us achieve gender equality in business and, most importantly, you need to actually do something about it in a real, substantive, concrete way.

You hear politicians constantly rolling out the old hack, "thoughts and prayers," applying the platitude to whatever tragedy is striking our country every day. "Thoughts and prayers" do not help a community devastated by a forest fire, hurricane, tornado, or an earthquake and living under the threat of the next one.

Consider the state of women in the corporate world today as its own kind of tragedy, because it is a real tragedy. And, just as the victims of a forest fire need help, that help is only as effective as the scale of concerted action being taken by those required to help. During a catastrophe of whatever sort, people need action, and they need it in the moment. A large element of that help is taking steps to prevent damage from occurring again and again. Well, the same can be said with gender equality in the workplace. The equivalent of "thoughts and prayers" for women in the workplace is, "we'll see about doing something about this, and we'll discuss this at the senior level and get back to you real soon."

Women are done with all the platitudes, done with the false promises, the false starts, and the bungled attempts. We have had more than enough of your "thoughts and prayers" for women in the workplace. How about "faith without works is dead?" One rings hollow, and the latter is wisdom for the ages.

I've presented a multitude of solutions in this book, so, for God's sake, please pick even one of these ideas and implement it in your workplace. At least it's a practical start. Once you take that first step, the remaining steps get easier and easier. I promise you that. But first, you need to own up to your part in all of this.

You guys need to stop treating C-suite and board positions like they are your God-given right. Stop spraying your territory like a dog at the park. This is a mindset that is an absolute killer for advancement in gender equality. We ARE already your equal—you don't seem to know that yet, so you are not treating us as such. Knowing and believing and behaving like we already are your equal is just a simple thought away. It doesn't require a forty-hour workshop. It's truly as simple as just thinking it and continuing to think it every minute you're at the office. No handwringing, no angst, no drama. Just simply think it because it is a fact, like day and night. Women are equal to men. Period.

And let's briefly talk about behavior in the workplace, okay? Women are not there to get your coffee. We are not there to find a husband. We are not there to be called "Honey," "Sweetheart," "Darling," or "Babe." We are not your pets. We are not your play toy. We are not there for you to hit on or refer to us as "Skirts." And it doesn't matter what the hell a woman is wearing; it is her choice to decide what she wears, just as you decide every day. YOUR responsibility is to keep your eyes and your hands to yourself and keep your comments civil and respectful. And if your momma didn't teach you how to treat women with respect, it's time to learn it now, or I promise your company, and possibly even you, will face the wrath of a thousand lawsuits. You can count on that. The office is absolutely not the place to let the teenage Lothario out unattended. It's not amusing. In fact, it's illegal, and I have no problem reminding you of that.

You may not understand that it's not fun to be on the receiving end of some men's less attractive social behaviors, but I assure you it is not. And it keeps women from advancing in their careers, which is absolutely un-acceptable. We are not a joke. Whether or not you can see that, it doesn't matter. Knock it off immediately. The women in your corporate office are now and forever off-limits to your male employees. I think that with the hard lessons of the *#MeToo* movement omnipresent, that reality should be self-evident. This discussion may have more than one facet, but once again, among them is that the behavior—the mindset that still believes these are part of the "office rules"—denigrates, intimidates, and tends to define a woman in a manner that impedes her ascension up the corporate ladder. Clear?

And just like the simple act of thinking women are already equal, that same principle applies to all of the outdated wives' tales you may still hold on to for dear life. Listen, guys, if we can carry around an ever-growing bowling ball in our uterus for forty weeks and then push that bowling ball through a mail slot, we are mentally tough enough, aggressive enough, and strong enough for a seat in the boardroom or C-suite corner office. You guys get a hangnail and you're out for a week, moaning and groaning about how excruciating the pain is! Freakin' amateurs. You guys have *no* idea what real pain is, so stop treating us like a weaker sex—fragile and thus second-class work partners. Not so, Sport. Bring it on.

And speaking of little humans, until you men truly share parental responsibilities, we will never achieve gender equality in the workplace. Just because she has a uterus doesn't mean she's responsible for all the diaper changes, feedings, bathing, cleaning, laundry, etc. In fact, because she carried YOUR child around inside her body, and she's the one who has to breastfeed or pump, it is all the MORE reason you guys need to get off your lazy behinds and help us out. It is only by doing so that you will gain a complete and visceral understanding of why we need a little more flexibility when we have a newborn or small child. So, take your parental leave when your partner does and share with them the workload at home. Only then will you be really ready to share leadership roles with women at work.

And probably the most important thing you guys need to do is talk less and listen more. Look, just because we don't want to behave like a bull in a China shop, interrupting fellow workers in a meeting, or we aren't the loudest person in the room doesn't mean we don't have something significant to add to the discussion. It's true that we don't necessarily behave like you guys do in a group setting, but you need to realize that is a good thing. Hearing other points of view, instead of trying to be "right" all of the time to impress your superiors, helps everyone achieve the desired corporate goals—making the company as successful as humanly possible. But when you ignore the few women in the room, you are facilitating the exact opposite of achieving company goals. I've said it a million times, more women in leadership equals higher profits for every company. The research supports that truth in spades. So, act more like us and less like you and we'll all make more money.

And just so you don't think I'm only picking on you men, I have a few things to say to women about our responsibility to help ourselves. We need to lose the "passivity behavior" that is ingrained in us. We need to speak up more, demand more, and do more to help ourselves reach the C-suites and boardrooms in our workplaces. And once there, demand lasting and permanent changes in gender equality where we work. We need to hold accountable those in leadership roles when it comes to gender equality. We need to demand more transparency regarding gender equality in our workplaces. And we need to demand fairness in our treatment and not stop until we achieve a parity and equity balance in our workplaces. I hope that what you have read in the preceding pages has affirmed for you that the sense you have of the disparity in the workplace is real, not imagined, and not at all unique to your circumstances. You have a voice that can be assertive, a voice that will be heard, a voice that should ring out against this last male bastion until we are heard and seen as gender equals.

However, we cannot readily achieve all of that without the support of our male coworkers. Gentlemen, you need to see that we are only asking what is due to us. Like you, we want to be seen, heard, appreciated, and given the same power within our workplaces that you have. We don't want to be given special treatment; we just want *equal* treatment and *equal* opportunities, the same kind of treatment you have always had. We're not asking for the moon; we just want our say and the power to effect change that will make our companies stronger and more successful and our lives more fulsome and rewarding.

So, either you're with us or you're against us. Either help us or get the hell out of our way. The Skirts are ready to rumble. The Suits better be ready.

ACKNOWLEDGMENTS

To my daughter, Ashley, who is one fierce force in business. Bootstrapping with you to create this gem, Smash+Tess—what a marvelous adventure! To call you my CEO makes Mama proud.

To my son, Adam, a courageous soul who has always made me feel celebrated in my career and provides insight into the minds of young men everywhere.

To the late Peter Podovinikoff, who served as mentor to me before we even knew what a mentor was. He taught me how to lead with elegance, warmth, and determination. I am better for having known and worked for him—twice.

To Tom Graham, the determined CEO who imported me from Canada and hired me to fill one of his key executive roles. I'll always be grateful for his unwavering support.

To John Antonio, the chair of the board who took a chance and championed me for president and CEO. His style, grace, mature thinking, and mindfulness have guided me for the past two decades.

To Dennis Ruffner, former chair of the board, who showed me the ropes at the board table and taught me so much about corporate America and the benefits of "no surprises."

To Roni Crichton, former chair of the board, who demonstrated such kindness and thoughtfulness in her management style. Her native intelligence and ability to articulate and explain any issue have been inspiring.

To the Women's Leadership Symposium—comprised of my very dear friends and colleagues. Let's just say it's my "super" network. I have learned so much from all of you.

To the best executive team ever—Marquis Boochee, Fabiana Burkett, Paris Chevalier, Kathryn Davis, Bertha Gascon, Todd Helmerson, Mary Roberts, Kelly Ritchey-Davoren, Mike Sacher, and Nicole Valentin-Smith. You were all unwavering in your support of "the big plans," and I will always be grateful for the lifetime friendships we created. And, of course, to my "stunt double," Lenora Nicholls, the best right-hand woman ever who allowed me to always be in three places at once.

To Joe Marich, my publicist who buoyed me up through the creation of this tome. I am grateful for your constant criticism and guidance.

To the intelligent and courageous leaders who have championed women into senior leadership roles, long before DEI said they should.

To all the amazing humans I have had the pleasure to work alongside during my career. You all have influenced my insights in this book. Thank you for the experiences and the teachings.

And lastly, to my husband, Doug, quietly the smartest person in any room, whose ever-critical eye has always been treasured by me. Thank you for the countless hours you contributed, you old white guy.

ENDNOTES

Chapter 2

Dixon-Fyle, Sundiatu, Kevin Dolan, Dame Vivian Hunt, and Sara Prince. "Diversity Wins: How Inclusion Matters." McKinsey & Company, April 6, 2022. https://www.mckinsey.com/featured-insights/diversity-and-inclusion/diversity-wins-how-inclusion-matters.

"Women in the Workplace 2021." McKinsey & Company, September 12, 2022. https://www.mckinsey.com/featured-insights/diversity-and-inclusion/women-in-the-workplace.

Hideg, Ivona, Anja Krstic, Raymond Trau, and Tanya Zarina. "Do Longer Maternity Leaves Hurt Women's Careers?" Harvard Business Review, September 13, 2021. https://hbr.org/2018/09/do-longer-maternity-leaves-hurt-womens-careers.

Maigua, Patrick. "Why Media Matters: Images of Women Scientists and Engineers." ITU Hub, December 1, 2021. https://www.itu.int/hub/2021/04/why-media-matters-images-of-women-scientists-and-engineers.

"Employment Characteristics of Families—2021 Working Mom Percentages." U.S. Bureau of Labor Statistics. https://www.bls.gov/news.release/pdf/famee.pdf.

Carpenter, Julia. "Women in the Fortune 500: 64 CEOS in Half a Century." CNNMoney. Cable News Network. https://money.cnn.com/interactive/pf/female-ceos-timeline/.

Johnson, Stefanie K., David R. Hekman, and Elsa T. Chan. "If There's Only One Woman in Your Candidate Pool, There's Statistically No Chance She'll Be Hired." Harvard Business Review, February 7, 2019. https://hbr.org/2016/04/if-theres-only-one-woman-in-your-candidate-pool-theres-statistically-no-chance-shell-be-hired.

"Chore Wars: Men, Women and Housework." National Science Foundation. https://www.nsf.gov/discoveries/disc_images.jsp?cntn_id=111458.

Burkus, David. "Everyone Likes Flex Time, But We Punish Women Who Use It." Harvard Business Review, August 31, 2021. https://hbr.org/2017/02/everyone-likes-flex-time-but-we-punish-women-who-use-it.

"Gender Equality in the U.S.—Assessing 500 Leading Companies on Workplace Equality Including Healthcare Benefits." Equileap, December 2020. https://equileap.com/wp-content/uploads/2020/12/Equileap_US_Report_2020.pdf.

Chapter 3

Zenger, Jack, and Joseph Folkman. "Research: Women Score Higher Than Men in Most Leadership Skills." Harvard Business Review, September 17, 2021. https://hbr.org/2019/06/research-women-score-higher-than-men-in-most-leadership-skills.

Tinsley, Catherine H., and Robin J. Ely. "What Most People Get Wrong About Men and Women." Harvard Business Review, November 19, 2019. https://hbr.org/2018/05/what-most-people-get-wrong-about-men-and-women.

Garikipati, Supriya, and Uma Kambhampati. "Leading the Fight Against the Pandemic: Does Gender 'Really' Matter?" SSRN, January 12, 2021. https://papers.ssrn.com/sol3/papers.cfm?abstract_id=3617953.

Blazina, Carrie. "Fast Facts on Views of Workplace Harassment amid Allegations against New York Gov. Cuomo." Pew Research Center, August 6, 2021. https://www.pewresearch.org/fact-tank/2021/08/06/fast-facts-on-views-of-workplace-harassment-amid-allegations-against-new-york-gov-cuomo/.

W. Brad Johnson, W. Brad, and David G. Smith. "Advancing Gender Equity as You Lead out of the Pandemic." Harvard Business Review, November 15, 2021. https://hbr.org/2021/10/advancing-gender-equity-as-you-lead-out-of-the-pandemic.

Shue, Kelly, and Ben Mattison. "Women Aren't Promoted Because Managers Underestimate Their Potential." Yale Insights, September 17, 2021. https://insights.som.yale.edu/insights/women-arent-promoted-because-managers-underestimate-their-potential.

Carter, Jacqueline. "The Secret to Women's Leadership That Can Drive Such a Positive Impact." Fast Company, March 22, 2022. https://www.fastcompany.com/90733328/the-secret-to-womens-leadership-that-can-drive-such-a-positive-impact.

Denend, Lyn, Paul Yock, and Dan Azagury. "Research: Small Wins Can Make a Big Impact on Gender Equality." Harvard Business Review, September 17, 2021. https://hbr.org/2020/11/research-small-wins-can-make-a-big-impact-on-gender-equality.

Makarov, Andrew. "How Overworking Affects Productivity." Monitask, August 12, 2021. https://www.monitask.com/en/blog/how-overworking-affects-productivity.

Ferrant, Gaëlle, Luca Maria Pesando, and Keiko Nowacka. "Unpaid Care Work: The Missing Link in the Analysis of Gender Gaps in Labour Outcomes." OECD Development Centre, December 2014. https://www.oecd.org/dev/development-gender/Unpaid_care_work.pdf.

Cooney, Samantha. "Vice President Pence Won't Eat Alone With Any Woman But His Wife Karen." TIME, March 29, 2017. https://time.com/4716439/mike-pence-karen-pence-eat-alone/.

Ely, Robin J., and Irene Padavic. "What's Really Holding Women Back?" Harvard Business Review, 2020. https://hbr.org/2020/03/whats-really-holding-women-back.

Dobbin, Frank, and Alexandra Kalev. "Why Sexual Harassment Programs Backfire." Harvard Business Review, 2020. https://hbr.org/2020/05/why-sexual-harassment-programs-backfire.

Chapter 4

Lorenzo, Rocio, and Martin Reeves. "How and Where Diversity Drives Financial Performance." Harvard Business Review, January 30, 2018. https://hbr.org/2018/01/how-and-where-diversity-drives-financial-performance.

Hansra, Navjot, Kellie McElhaney, and Genevieve Smith. "The Business Case for Gender Diversity." UC Berkeley HAAS School of Business, June 2019. https://haas.berkeley.edu/wp-content/uploads/Business-Case-for-Gender-Diversity_EGAL_June-2019.pdf.

Martinelli, Katherine. "How Millennials Are Solving the Workplace Diversity Problem." Duke Office for Institutional Equity, October 18, 2018. https://oie.duke.edu/how-millennials-are-solving-workplace-diversity-problem.

Hamlin, Jessica. "The Diversity Premium: More Women, Higher Returns." Institutional Investor, September 28, 2021. https://www.institutionalinvestor.com/article/b1tshzrjw8fqhk/The-Diversity-Premium-More-Women-Higher-Returns.

Lydon, Tom. "Corporate Board Gender Diversity Improving, Says Moody's." ETF Trends, February 23, 2022. https://www.etftrends.com/esg-channel/corporate-board-gender-diversity-improving-says-moodys/.

"The Female Millennial." PwC. https://www.pwc.com/gx/en/women-at-pwc/internationalwomensday/assets/a-new-era-of-talent-report.pdf.

"What Is the Impact of Gender Diversity on Technology Business Performance." National Center for Women & Information Technology. https://wpassets.ncwit. org/wp-content/uploads/2021/05/13195341/impactgenderdiversitytechbusinessperformance_print.pdf.

"Women on Boards: Global Trends in Gender Diversity." MSCI, November 30, 2015. https://www.msci.com/www/research-paper/research-insight-women -on/0263428390.

"Fresh Copy: How Ursula Burns Reinvented Xerox." Fast Company, November 19, 2011. https://www.fastcompany.com/1793533/fresh-copy-how-ursula-burn s-reinvented-xerox.

Herring, Cedric. "Does Diversity Pay?: Race, Gender, and the Business Case for Diversity." SAGE Journals, April 1, 2009. https://journals.sagepub.com/doi/ abs/10.1177/000312240907400203.

Sayeh, Antoinette M. "Gender-Balanced Leadership: Guarding Financial Stability in Crisis Times." IMF Communications Department, June 10, 2020. https://www. imf.org/en/News/Articles/2020/06/10/sp061020-gender-balanced-leadershi p-guarding-financial-stability-in-crisis-times.

Chapter 5

"New US Study Reveals Gap in Intention Versus Action When It Comes to Male Allyship for Gender Equality." Equimundo, March 8, 2019. https://www.equimundo.org/new-us-study-male-allyship-for-gender-equality/.

Ammerman, Colleen, and Boris Groysberg. "The Secret to Getting More Women in Leadership: Men." Newsweek Magazine, April 7, 2021. https://www.newsweek. com/2021/04/16/secret-getting-more-women-leadership-men-1581437.html.

Kerr, Geoffrey, and Alix Pollack. "Engaging Men: Barriers and Gender Norms (Report)." Catalyst, January 19, 2022. https://www.catalyst.org/research/ engaging-men-barriers-norms/.

Paquette, Danielle. "Sexism Is over, According to Most Men." The Washington Post, August 22, 2016. https://www.washingtonpost.com/news/wonk/ wp/2016/08/22/sexism-is-over-according-to-most-men/.

"Women, Leadership, and Missed Opportunities." IBM. https://www.ibm.com/ thought-leadership/institute-business-value/report/women-leadership-2021.

"Women in the Workplace 2018." LeanIn.Org and McKinsey & Company. https://womenintheworkplace.com/2018.

Sue, Derald Wing. *Microaggressions in Everyday Life: Race, Gender, and Sexual Orientation*. Hoboken, NJ: Wiley, 2010.

"25% Of Women in the Workplace Endure 'Frequent' Sexist Incidents." Yahoo! Finance. Perceptyx, March 22, 2022. https://nz.finance.yahoo.com/news/25-women-workplace-endure-frequent-130000837.html.

Alaimo, Kara. "Justice Sonia Sotomayor Deals with 'Manterruptions,' Too. Here's How We Can Stop Them." CNN: Cable News Network, October 19, 2021. https://www.cnn.com/2021/10/18/opinions/sonia-sotomayor-manterruptions-alaimo/index.html.

Snyder, Kieran. "How to Get Ahead as a Woman in Tech: Interrupt Men." Slate Magazine, July 23, 2014. https://slate.com/human-interest/2014/07/study-men-interrupt-women-more-in-tech-workplaces-but-high-ranking-women-learn-to-interrupt.html.

Huddleston, Charles, and Nelson Mullins Riley. "How Men Unwittingly Display Disrespect to Female Colleagues at Work—And Some Suggestions on How to Fix This Problem." Nelson Mullins Riley & Scarborough LLP, March 15, 2022. https://www.jdsupra.com/legalnews/how-men-unwittingly-display-disrespect-7113298/.

Annis, Barbara, and John Gray. "Are Women Being Excluded?" U.S. Chamber of Commerce Foundation, November 25, 2013. https://www.uschamberfoundation.org/blog/post/are-women-being-excluded.

Ziv, Stav. "The 'Elephant in [Silicon] Valley': Women in Tech." Newsweek, January 15, 2016. https://www.newsweek.com/silicon-valley-women-tech-survey-416206.

Wensil, Brenda F., and Kathryn Heath. "4 Ways Women Can Build Relationships When They Feel Excluded at Work." Harvard Business Review, July 17, 2015. https://hbr.org/2018/07/4-ways-women-can-build-relationships-when-they-feel-excluded-at-work.

Mayer, David M. "How Not to Advocate for a Woman at Work." Harvard Business Review, July 26, 2017. https://hbr.org/2017/07/how-not-to-advocate-for-a-woman-at-work.

Macke, Erin, Gabriela Gall Rosa, Shannon Gilmartin, and Caroline Simard. "Assignments Are Critical Tools to Achieve Workplace Gender Equity." MIT Sloan Management Review, January 4, 2022. https://sloanreview.mit.edu/article/assignments-are-critical-tools-to-achieve-workplace-gender-equity/.

"Women in Leadership: Tackling Corporate Culture from the Top." Rockefeller Foundation. https://www.rockefellerfoundation.org/wp-content/uploads/Women-in-Leadership-Tackling-Corporate-Culture-from-the-Top.pdf.

Krisch, Joshua A. "Are Most Men Sexist? The Data Says Yes Even If They Say No." Yahoo! Life, December 26, 2018. https://www.yahoo.com/lifestyle/most-men-sexist-data-says-173859699.html.

Brescoll, Victoria L., and Eric Luis Uhlmann. "Can an Angry Woman Get Ahead?: Status Conferral, Gender, and Expression of Emotion in the Workplace." Gender Action Portal. https://gap.hks.harvard.edu/can-angry-woman-get-ahead-status-conferral-gender-and-expression-emotion-workplace.

"Attitudes toward Women in the Workplace." Ipsos. https://www.ipsos.com/sites/default/files/ct/news/documents/2022-03/2022%20Ipsos%20Tracking%20-%20Core%20Political%20Presidential%20Approval%20Tracker%2028%20Feb%20thru%201%20Mar%202022.pdf.

Williams, Joan C., Denise Lewin Loyd, Mikayla Boginsky, and Frances Armas-Edwards. "How One Company Worked to Root Out Bias from Performance Reviews." Harvard Business Review, April 21, 2021. https://hbr.org/2021/04/how-one-company-worked-to-root-out-bias-from-performance-reviews.

Chapter 6

Hauck, Carley. "Nine Tips for Being a Male Ally at Work." Greater Good Magazine, May 19, 2021. https://greatergood.berkeley.edu/article/item/nine_tips_for_being_a_male_ally_at_work.

Krentz, Matt, Olivier Wierzba, Katie Abouzahr, Jennifer Garcia-Alonso, and Frances Brooks Taplett. "Five Ways Men Can Improve Gender Diversity at Work." BCG Global, October 10, 2017. https://www.bcg.com/publications/2017/people-organization-behavior-culture-five-ways-men-improve-gender-diversity-work.

"Five Simple Ways to Be a Better Male Ally." JPMorgan Chase & Co. https://www.jpmorganchase.com/news-stories/5-simple-ways-to-be-a-better-male-ally.

Godoy, Jody. "California Law Requiring Women on Company Boards Struck Down." Thomson Reuters, May 17, 2022. https://www.reuters.com/legal/legalindustry/california-law-requiring-women-company-boards-struck-down-2022-05-16/.

"50/50 Women on Boards Gender Diversity Directory." Directory: 50/50 Women on Boards. https://5050wob.com/directory/.

Rowley, Connagh. "Q2 2022 Equilar Gender Diversity Index." Equilar, September 8, 2022. https://www.equilar.com/reports/96-q2-2022-equilar-gender-diversity-index.

"Women of Color in the United States (Quick Take)." Catalyst, January 31, 2022. https://www.catalyst.org/research/women-of-color-in-the-united-states/.

"Publications Archive: Women's Fund of Rhode Island." Women's Fund of Rhode Island. https://wfri.org/research/.

"Census Bureau Releases New Educational Attainment Data." US Census Bureau, February 24, 2022. https://www.census.gov/newsroom/press-releases/2022/educational-attainment.html.

"Women @ Work 2022: A Global Outlook." Deloitte Touche Tohmatsu Limited. https://www2.deloitte.com/content/dam/Deloitte/global/Documents/deloitte-women-at-work-2022-a-global-outlook.pdf.

Moser, Charlotte E. "Male Allies at Work: Gender-Equality Supportive Men Reduce Negative Underrepresentation Effects Among Women." SAGE Journals, August 9, 2021. https://journals.sagepub.com/doi/abs/10.1177/19485506211033748?journalCode=sppa.

Cox, Josie. "Paternity Leave: The Hidden Barriers Keeping Men at Work." BBC Worklife, July 12, 2021. https://www.bbc.com/worklife/article/20210712-paternity-leave-the-hidden-barriers-keeping-men-at-work.

Chapter 7

"Unilever Full Year Results 2021." Unilever PLC, September 2, 2022. https://www.unilever.com/news/press-and-media/press-releases/2022/unilever-full-year-results-2021/.

"Sodexo—Making Every Day Count: Driving Business Success through the Employee Experience (Practices)." Catalyst, January 1, 2012. https://www.catalyst.org/research/sodexo-making-every-day-count-driving-business-success-through-the-employee-experience/.

DiversityInc Staff. "Businesses Must Enter 'Gender-Balance Zone'." DiversityInc Best Practices, April 1, 2020. https://www.diversityincbestpractices.com/businesses-must-enter-gender-balance-zone/.

"A Surprising Way to Increase Profits by 10–15%." Sodexo Group, January 2, 2020. https://www.sodexo.com/inspired-thinking/gender-increasing-profit-in-fm.html.

Buzalka, Mike. "Sodexo Names Sophie Bellon CEO." Food Management, February 17, 2022. https://www.food-management.com/news-trends/sodexo-names-sophie-bellon-ceo.

"Gender Equality in the Workplace." Accenture. https://www.accenture.com/za-en/about/inclusion-diversity/gender-equality.

"Achieving Progress towards Gender Parity at Global Leadership." PwC. https://www.heforshe.org/sites/default/files/2021-05/hfs_proven_solutions_pwc.pdf.

"Blind Spots." PwC. https://www.pwc.com/us/en/about-us/blind-spots.html.

"The Myth of Flexibility for Women in the Workplace." World Economic Forum, May 16, 2022. https://www.weforum.org/agenda/2022/05/the-myth-of-flexibility-for-women-in-the-workplace.

Hyder, Brent. "2022 Equal Pay Update: The Salesforce Approach to Pay Fairness." Salesforce News, March 30, 2022. https://www.salesforce.com/news/stories/2022-equal-pay-update-the-salesforce-approach-to-pay-fairness/.

Beniof, Marc, and Monica Langley. "How Salesforce Closed the Pay Gap Between Men and Women." Wired, October 15, 2019. https://www.wired.com/story/how-salesforce-closed-pay-gap-between-men-women/.

"Medtronic: Igniting Women to Lead Through the Medtronic Women's Network (Practices)." Catalyst, March 12, 2020. https://www.catalyst.org/research/medtronic-igniting-women-network/.

Vomhof Jr., John. "Parity.org Names Best Buy One of 'Best Companies for Women to Advance'." Best Buy Corporate News and Information, June 22, 2021. https://corporate.bestbuy.com/parity-org-names-best-buy-one-of-best-companies-for-women-to-advance/.

Vaghul, Kavya. "A Small Fraction of Corporations Share Diversity Data, but Disclosure Is Rapidly on the Rise." JUST Capital, January 19, 2021. https://just-capital.com/news/a-small-fraction-of-corporations-share-diversity-data-but-disclosure-is-rapidly-on-the-rise/.

McCann, Bailey. "Investors Telling Managers: Show Your Progress." Pensions & Investments, April 25, 2022. https://www.pionline.com/special-report-diversity-equity-inclusion/investors-have-message-managers-show-your-progress.

Dobbin, Frank, and Alexandra Kalev. "Why Diversity Programs Fail." Harvard Business Review, 2016. https://hbr.org/2016/07/why-diversity-programs-fail.

"Gender Equality Global Report & Ranking." Equileap. https://equileap.com/wp-content/uploads/2022/03/Equileap_Global_Report_2022.pdf.

Sweet, Joni. "History of Women in the Workplace." Stacker, October 25, 2021. https://stacker.com/stories/4393/history-women-workplace.

Vaghul, Kavya. "Just Over Half of the Largest U.S. Companies Share Workforce Diversity Data as Calls for Transparency from Investors and Regulators Grow." JUST Capital, February 6, 2022. https://justcapital.com/reports/share-of-larges t-us-companies-disclosing-race-and-ethnicity-data-rises/.

Chapter 8

Thomas, Daniel, and Ian Smith. "Male Managers in UK Block Gender Balance Efforts, Research Suggests." Financial Times, May 16, 2022. https://www. ft.com/content/022eecef-940f-453c-aaa9-eeabec83aa28.

Rogish, Alison, Stacy Sandler, and Neda Shemluck. "Women in the C-Suite." Deloitte Insights, March 4, 2020. https://www2.deloitte.com/us/en/insights/ industry/financial-services/women-in-the-c-suite.htm.

Golden, Ryan. "Female CHROs at Top Public Companies Outnumber, Outearn Male Counterparts." HR Dive, October 29, 2021. https://www.hrdive.com/ news/female-chros-at-top-public-companies-outnumber-outearn-male-counterparts/609157/.

Almog, Gal. "5 Ways to Fix Your Diversity, Equity, and Inclusion Program." Fast Company, September 8, 2021. https://www.fastcompany.com/90673391/5-way s-to-fix-your-diversity-equity-and-inclusion-program.

"Women, Leadership, and Missed Opportunities." IBM.

Marchant, Natalie. "Zurich Added These 6 Words to Job Adverts and More Women Applied." World Economic Forum, December 8, 2020. https://www.weforum. org/agenda/2020/12/zurich-flexible-working-women-diversity/.

Bleiweis, Robin. "Why Salary History Bans Matter to Securing Equal Pay." Center for American Progress, March 24, 2021. https://www.americanprogress.org/ article/salary-history-bans-matter-securing-equal-pay/.

"Salary History Bans." HR Dive, February 3, 2022. https://www.hrdive.com/news/ salary-history-ban-states-list/516662/.

Zalis, Shelley. "You Need to Be a Workplace Champion for Gender Equity. Here's How." Fast Company, November 19, 2021. https://www.fastcom-pany.com/90697767/you-need-to-be-a-workplace-champion-for-gender-equ ity-heres-how.

Sokol, Stephanie. "A Guide to Maternity Leave Laws by State: Know Your Rights." FamilyEducation, April 23, 2022. https://www.familyeducation.com/ pregnancy/maternity-leave/maternity-leave-laws-what-are-your-rights.

Schroeder-Saulnier, Debora. "To Retain Women, U.S. Companies Need Better Childcare Policies." Harvard Business Review, May 28, 2021. https://hbr.org/2021/05/to-retain-women-u-s-companies-need-better-childcare-policies.

Collins, Caitlyn, Leah Ruppanner, and William J. Scarborough. "Why Haven't U.S. Mothers Returned to Work? The Child-Care Infrastructure They Need Is Still Missing." The Washington Post, November 8, 2021. https://www.washingtonpost.com/politics/2021/11/08/why-havent-us-mothers-returned-work-child-care-infrastructure-they-need-is-still-missing/.

"National Single Parent Day: March 21, 2022." US Census Bureau, March 21, 2022. https://www.census.gov/newsroom/stories/single-parent-day.html.

Spiggle, Tom. "Eight Laws That Helped Women Make History in the Workforce." Forbes Magazine, March 13, 2019. https://www.forbes.com/sites/tomspiggle/2019/03/13/8-laws-that-helped-women-make-history-in-the-workforce/.

Covert, Bryce. "The Secret to Getting More Women on Corporate Boards: The $100,000 Threat." POLITICO Magazine, February 25, 2022. https://www.politico.com/news/magazine/2022/02/25/california-companies-women-boards-quotas-00010745.

Nagele-Piazza, Lisa. "Can a Company Be Required to Have a Diverse Board of Directors?" SHRM, January 12, 2022. https://www.shrm.org/resourcesandtools/legal-and-compliance/state-and-local-updates/pages/calif-diverse-board-of-directors.aspx.

Griffith, Erin. "California Law Requiring Board Diversity Is Struck Down." The New York Times, April 3, 2022. https://www.nytimes.com/2022/04/03/business/california-board-diversity-law.html.

Gormley, Todd A., Vishal K. Gupta, David A. Matsa, Sandra Mortal, and Lukai Yang. "Companies Are Adding More Women to Their Boards. What's Driving the Change?" Kellogg Insight, May 3, 2021. https://insight.kellogg.northwestern.edu/article/women-company-boards.

Gormley, Todd A., Vishal K. Gupta, David A. Matsa, Sandra Mortal, and Lukai Yang. "The Big Three and Board Gender Diversity: The Effectiveness of Shareholder Voice." SSRN, July 31, 2021. https://papers.ssrn.com/sol3/papers.cfm?abstract_id=3724653.

Hendrickson, Christine. "Pay Transparency, Pay Equity, Salary History— What's New for 2022." Bloomberg Law, January 24, 2022. https://news.bloomberglaw.com/daily-labor-report/pay-transparency-pay-equity-salary-history-whats-new-for-2022.

Peterson, Randall S., Gillian Ku, Herminia Ibarra, and Eliot Sherman. "Women at Work Championing Change through Research." London Business School, March 9, 2018. https://www.london.edu/think/women-at-work-championing-change-through-research.

Green, Jeff. "Male Executives Control 99 Times More S&P 500 Shares Than Women." Bloomberg, June 6, 2022. https://www.bloomberg.com/news/articles/2022-06-06/male-executives-control-99-times-more-s-p-500-shares-than-women.

Tappin, Steve. "What Female CEOs in Thailand Can Teach the 96% of Male CEOs in Fortune 500." LinkedIn, April 26, 2016. https://www.linkedin.com/pulse/what-female-ceos-thailand-can-teach-96-male-fortune-500-steve-tappin/.

de Yonge, John. "Has Your C-Suite Changed to Reflect the Changing Times?" EY Knowledge, September 24, 2019. https://www.ey.com/en_us/growth/has-your-c-suite-changed-to-reflect-the-changing-times.

Chapter 9

Lodewick, Colin. "Pay for Women CEOs Rose 26% Last Year. But We're Still Far from Gender Equity in Top Corporate Positions." Fortune, May 26, 2022. https://fortune.com/2022/05/26/pay-for-women-ceos-rose-26-last-year-but-were-still-far-from-gender-equity-in-top-corporate-roles/.

Centola, Damon, Joshua Becker, Devon Brackbill, and Andrea Baronchelli. "Experimental Evidence for Tipping Points in Social Convention." Science, June 8, 2018. https://www.science.org/doi/10.1126/science.aas8827.

Vadgama, Anam. "Companies Changing Cultures: The Power of Pledges!" The Life You Can Save, February 28, 2020. https://www.thelifeyoucansave.org/blog/companies-changing-cultures-the-power-of-pledges.

Amazon Staff. "The Climate Pledge Announces Nearly 100 New Signatories." Amazon, March 14, 2022. https://www.aboutamazon.com/news/sustainability/the-climate-pledge-announces-nearly-100-new-signatories.

ACCP Staff. "Corporate Response to the Crisis in Ukraine." Association of Corporate Citizenship Professionals, June 6, 2022. https://accp.org/resources/csr-resources/accp-insights-blog/corporate-response-to-the-crisis-in-ukraine/.

Chintagunta, Pradeep K., Yogesh Kansal, and Pradeep Pachigolla. "In Corporate Responses to Black Lives Matter, Commitment Speaks Volumes." The University of Chicago Booth School of Business, August 13, 2020. https://www.

chicagobooth.edu/review/corporate-responses-black-lives-matter-commitmen t-speaks-volumes.

Walker, Bryan, and Sarah A. Soule. "Changing Company Culture Requires a Movement, Not a Mandate." Harvard Business Review, June 20, 2017. https://hbr. org/2017/06/changing-company-culture-requires-a-movement-not-a-mandate.

"Shaping the Sustainable Organization." Accenture | World Economic Forum. https://www.accenture.com/us-en/insights/sustainability/ sustainable-organization?c=acn_glb_buildingsustainworldeconomic- fo_12781500&n=otc_0122.

Hashempour, Parisa. "Gender Parity Is 135 Years Away, Unless We Speed up Progress in Politics and Economics, According to a World Economic Forum Panel." Business Insider, May 26, 2022. https://www.businessinsider.com/gender-parit y-requires-prioritizing-political-and-economic-empowerment-2022-5.

CPSIA information can be obtained
at www.ICGtesting.com
Printed in the USA
LVHW070729010323
740644LV00023B/1310